# THE ILLUSTRATED
# A to Z
# GUIDE TO
# BIBLE
# PEOPLE

# THE ILLUSTRATED
# A TO Z
# GUIDE TO
# BIBLE
# PEOPLE

*180 Easy-Reading Entries,*
*from Aaron to Zipporah*

## CHRISTOPHER D. HUDSON

BARBOUR
PUBLISHING

Content produced by Christopher D. Hudson, Hudson Bible. Entries previously published in *Fascinating People of the Bible.*

ISBN 978-1-62836-008-0

Cover images: man—Shutterstock; caravan—Shutterstock; woman holding basket—Keren Su/Lonely Planet Images/Getty

Published by Barbour Publishing, Inc., P.O. Box 719, Uhrichsville, Ohio 44683, www.barbourbooks.com

*Our mission is to publish and distribute inspirational products offering exceptional value and biblical encouragement to the masses.*

Member of the
Evangelical Christian
Publishers Association

# CONTENTS

# INTRODUCTION

*Therefore, since we are surrounded by so great a cloud of witnesses,
let us also lay aside every weight and the sin that clings so closely,
and let us run with perseverance the race that is set before us.*

HEBREWS 12:1 NRSV

Bible studies and Sunday school classes can fill our minds with many important facts. Through them we learn names of cities, recount historical events, and memorize favorite verses. And though every bit of Bible knowledge we learn can be worthwhile, sometimes we forget one of the most basic characteristics of the Bible: that it's a book about people.

Though these men and women lived thousands of years before us, we share a similar human journey. Together we enjoy the pleasures of life and learn to look to God when faced with devastating pain. Along with them, we experience the excitement of young love, the challenges of raising a family, and the complexities of trying to live for God in a fallen world.

Separated by centuries, we're still joined by a common human spirit—and we serve a God who spans the ages. As we live in our modern communities, we have the opportunity to learn from those who have gone before us—both from the good and from the bad.

*The Illustrated A to Z Guide to Bible People* contains brief biographies of 180 individuals or people groups of scripture—women and men, good and bad, weak and powerful, honorable and worthy of disdain. There are more than three thousand individuals named in scripture—in addition to unnamed persons and people groups—so this book only scratches the surface of their stories. Some of the names you'll encounter in the following pages are very familiar, while others may be unknown to you. But all of them were included in God's Word as examples for us today.

Each entry also includes a brief, bonus sidebar:

- Interesting. . . : a "did you know?"-style factoid
- Information: an additional detail on the person or persons profiled
- Insight: a spiritual point you can apply to your own life

I pray that as you read the stories of these lives, you will find your own life changed as well.

Christopher D. Hudson
@ReadEngageApply.com
facebook.com/Christopher.D.Hudon.books

AARON wears the high priest's breastplate and carries a censer in this statue in a Roman basilica.

# AARON
## Brother of Moses

*Now if perfection was through the Levitical priesthood (for on the basis of it the people received the Law), what further need was there for another priest to arise according to the order of Melchizedek, and not be designated according to the order of Aaron?*

HEBREWS 7:11 NASB

Ordinary leaders often become remarkable leaders because of extraordinary support. While Moses was arguably the greatest Hebrew leader during Bible times, much of his success came with the help of his brother, Aaron. Aaron stood alongside Moses as they confronted Pharaoh, and he compensated for Moses' weakness by often serving as Moses' spokesperson (see Exodus 4:10). And though Moses served as the principal leader of the Hebrew people, Aaron also held an important position of influence.

It was Aaron's staff that became a snake before Pharaoh (Exodus 7:10). That same staff also turned Egypt's water into blood (Exodus 7:19), brought frogs on the Egyptians (Exodus 8:5), and caused gnats to swarm the Egyptians (Exodus 8:16). Aaron and his sons became the first Hebrew priests appointed by God (Exodus 28:3). The significance of their role as intermediaries between God and the Hebrews became clearly evidenced when they interceded for the people after the rebellion of Korah, Dathan, and Abiram (Numbers 16).

While Aaron usually provided loyal assistance to Moses, he also experienced some notable failures as a supporter. For example, Aaron and his sister, Miriam, received a sound reprimand from God when they spoke against Moses for marrying a Cushite (Numbers 12:1–15). On another occasion, Aaron buckled under the pressure of the people and created a golden calf while Moses communed with God away from the camp (Exodus 32). As the people approached the Promised Land, Aaron died at the age of 123 on Mount Hor (Numbers 33:39).

INSIGHT: Though generally a good priest, Aaron's imperfection became an important theological symbol. In spite of faithful service to the people of God, Hebrew priests could not provide the perfect intercession required to obtain God's complete forgiveness. Their service illustrated the need for something more, something better. God met that need through the perfect priesthood initiated by Jesus Christ (see Hebrews 5:4; 7:11).

# ABDON
## Judge of Israel

He had forty sons and thirty grandsons, who rode on seventy donkeys.
He led Israel eight years.
JUDGES 12:14

It's often what *isn't* mentioned that really tells the story. For example, if someone filling out a job application fails to answer why he or she left a previous job, it's very likely that this information would make the applicant look bad. It's hard to say for sure, but the Bible's short record of Abdon may be saying as much by what it doesn't say as by what it says.

The Bible does make it clear, though, that Abdon must have been a very wealthy man. It is impressive enough that he could have fathered and raised forty sons, but it is a truly incredible achievement to provide each of them—as well as each of his thirty grandsons—with his own donkey to ride. To connect that to today, it would be like saying he bought each of them his own car!

But curiously absent from his record is any mention of his deeds or of Israel's deliverance from any oppressing nation. That may be because he never really performed any amazing deeds or helped to rescue Israel from anyone. He may have simply been the most influential person around when the nation needed to fill the role of judge. We don't know for sure, but that seems to be the implication from the Bible's account (Judges 12:13–15).

INFORMATION: Abdon came from the town of Pirathon in the hill country of Ephraim. This otherwise unknown town was also the home of Benaiah, the head of David's bodyguard (2 Samuel 23:30).

# ABEL
## Son of Adam and Eve

Abel also brought of the firstborn of his flock and of their fat portions.
And the LORD had regard for Abel and his offering.
GENESIS 4:4 ESV

Abel became the world's first victim to violent crime. The son of Adam and Eve, Abel died at the hands of his older brother Cain. Before this fateful day, Abel lived in a small human village made up only of his own family. As a family might do in this scenario, they divided the jobs among different members: Cain farmed the earth and Abel cared for the herds of animals.

During the course of time, the two brothers offered a sacrifice to God. Abel offered his gift from his herds and Cain from his fields. While we can't know for certain the reason God accepted one sacrifice and not the other, the biblical narrative reveals that Abel's offering obtained God's approval. Cain, on the other hand, received a reprimand. While we don't have further details of the story, we see into Cain's heart through his next action: the murder of his brother. The anger and jealousy in Cain's heart may have been the exact reason God had rejected his sacrifice. In contrast, Hebrews 11:4 records, "By faith Abel offered to God a more acceptable sacrifice than Cain, through which he was commended as righteous, God commending him by accepting his gifts. And through his faith, though he died, he still speaks" (ESV).

While there has been much speculation about the nature of the two sacrifices, it may simply be that Abel's act of worship was offered by faith and Cain's was offered with an angry spirit of jealousy and obligation.

INSIGHT: There are many reasons to attend and get involved in church. Even steps taken to grow in your spiritual life can be cloaked with spiritual reasons that mask a concern for appearances or the need to match other people's expectations. The jealous need for acceptance and approval can result in your doing good activities like Cain—but doing them without the heart motivation of which God approves.

# ABIGAIL
## Nabal's Widow and David's Wife

David said to Abigail, "Praise be to the LORD, the God of Israel, who has sent you today to meet me. May you be blessed for your good judgment and for keeping me from bloodshed this day and from avenging myself with my own hands."
1 SAMUEL 25:32-33

Everyone has needed an Abigail at some point in life—someone who, through discretion and grace, has kept us from doing something we would really regret. Abigail was the wife of a wealthy herder named Nabal, whose name means "fool." While David was on the run from Saul, he spent some time in the area near Nabal's flocks and kept them safe from potential thieves. When the time came for Nabal's sheep to be sheared, David sent his men to receive some payment for their services, but Nabal rebuffed them and sent them away empty-handed. When David heard about this, he was furious and gathered his men to go kill every one of Nabal's men.

But Abigail, whom the Bible describes as discerning and beautiful, intercepted David before he reached Nabal's men, offered him some food, and persuaded him to turn back from repaying Nabal for his affront.

David immediately recognized the wisdom in Abigail's words, turned back from his vengeance, and praised God for using Abigail to save him from doing something he would have regretted (1 Samuel 25).

When Abigail informed her husband of all that transpired between her and David, Nabal's "heart failed him and he became like a stone" (1 Samuel 25:37). Ten days later Nabal died, and David took Abigail as his wife.

INFORMATION: David once had to rescue Abigail and one of his other wives from the Amalekites, who had raided his town of Ziklag and carried off many people (1 Samuel 30).

Two hundred loaves of bread, five dressed sheep, and two bottles of wine—ABIGAIL's peace offering to an angry David.

# ABIMELECH
## King of Gerar

From there Abraham journeyed toward the territory of the Negeb
and lived between Kadesh and Shur; and he sojourned in Gerar.
And Abraham said of Sarah his wife, "She is my sister."
And Abimelech king of Gerar sent and took Sarah.
GENESIS 20:1-2 ESV

We aren't doing people any favors when we bow to fear and withhold the truth
from them. In fact, we may be putting them in harm's way. Just ask Abimelech.
Abimelech was the king of Gerar in southern Canaan during the time Abraham
lived there. When Abraham moved into the area, he knew that someone might
take an interest in his wife, Sarah—and he feared that he might be killed so that
she could be taken. So Abraham told a half-truth (or rather, a partial lie) that Sarah
was his sister. But he hid the fact that she was also his wife, and he told Sarah to
tell people that he was her brother. So Abimelech took her with the intent to make
her his wife.

But before Abimelech even touched her, the Lord warned him that Sarah
was already married and that he must return her to Abraham—or die. So Abimelech sent Sarah back to Abraham right away and paid him a large sum to
account for any guilt he had incurred by his actions. He also invited Abraham to
live anywhere in his land.

INSIGHT: Abraham lied about Sarah because he thought the
people of Gerar did not fear God. Yet Abraham's dishonesty and fear
revealed his own lack of fear of God and his selfish concern for his
own well-being. If Abraham had trusted God to watch over him and
was truthful from the beginning, he would not have unnecessarily
endangered Abimelech's life and well-being.

# ABIRAM, KORAH, AND DATHAN
## Led a Revolt against Moses

Now Korah the son of Izhar, son of Kohath, son of Levi, and Dathan and Abiram
the sons of Eliab, and On the son of Peleth, sons of Reuben, took men. And
they rose up before Moses, with a number of the people of Israel, 250 chiefs
of the congregation, chosen from the assembly, well-known men.
NUMBERS 16:1–2 ESV

It's not every day the earth swallows up rebellious people. God clearly wanted to
make a statement when He chose this as the punishment for Korah, Abiram, and
Dathan. These three men, their families, and their followers reaped an unusual,
but deserved, judgment for their insolence against God and Moses.

While Korah had a faithful following of 250 men, all three of these men held
leadership roles in the Hebrew community. Yet Korah, a Levite, and the two brothers,
Abiram and Dathan (from the tribe of Reuben), were jealous of Moses' unique leadership and the special relationship he shared with God. They envied Aaron's position
as priest to the people. This led them to incite the people to rebel against Moses and
grumble against Aaron. Their charge: "For all in the congregation are holy, every one
of them, and the Lord is among them. Why then do you exalt yourselves above the
assembly of the Lord?" (Numbers 16:3 ESV). They failed to find contentment in what
God had already given them, complaining instead that they wanted more.

Though Moses and Aaron interceded for these rebellious people (Numbers
16:22), God caused the earth to open underneath the three men, their families,
and some of their followers. The remaining followers of Korah were destroyed by
fire from heaven (Numbers 16:35).

Even after witnessing this supernatural execution, the people were slow to
refocus their devotion to God and His appointed leaders—Moses and Aaron. Less
than twenty-four hours later, the people of Israel rallied against Moses and Aaron
and blamed them for the dramatic death of their popular community leaders. God
acted again, sending a plague to strike down the entire assembly of people. When
Moses and Aaron intervened on behalf of the people, God stopped the plague—
but by that time it had already killed nearly fifteen thousand.

INTERESTING. . . These rebels, particularly Dathan and Korah,
became symbols and archetypes of rebellious behavior throughout
Israel's history. (See Numbers 26:9–10; Deuteronomy 11:6; Psalm
106:17.)

# ABRAHAM
## Patriarch of Israel

The LORD had said to Abram, "Go from your country, your people
and your father's household to the land I will show you. I will
make you into a great nation, and I will bless you;
I will make your name great, and you will be a blessing."
GENESIS 12:1-2

Abraham is a paragon of faith. He lived in a world that regarded family and tribe as security, but the Lord called him to leave his family, people, and country and travel to a different land—and Abraham did so without question! The land that the Lord was going to give Abraham's descendants was already well settled, so how could he "inherit" this land? Finally, his wife was in her sixties—well past childbearing years—so how could he ever expect to have any descendants at all (Genesis 12)?

But Abraham trusted God and His promises, and his faith was rewarded. Abraham and Sarah eventually bore Isaac, who fathered Jacob, who fathered the leaders of the twelve tribes of Israel. Many years later, the Israelites conquered the Promised Land of Canaan and occupied it as their inheritance. God was indeed faithful.

Abraham was not without his times of doubt. For instance, on two separate occasions he lied about his wife in order to protect his life (Genesis 12, 20). Abraham also expressed doubt that he would bear a son to carry on his name and estate (Genesis 15:1–3). Nevertheless, when the Lord made promises to Abraham, he "believed the LORD, and he credited it to him as righteousness" (Genesis 15:6).

INSIGHT: While Abraham is certainly a great example of faith for Christians today, that is not all he is to us. We are also his very children, the descendants whom God had promised to give him and to bless. Paul makes this clear in his letter to the Galatians: "Understand, then, that those who have faith are children of Abraham" (Galatians 3:7). Thank God that all His faithful promises are made available even to us who believe Him today.

In a time when a man's success was measured by the size of the family he supported, ABRAHAM must have been daunted and humbled when God promised his family would be more numerous than the grains of sand on the shore or the stars in the sky.

# ABSALOM
## Son of David

Then Absalom sent secret messengers throughout the tribes of Israel to say,
"As soon as you hear the sound of the trumpets, then say,
'Absalom is king in Hebron.'"
2 SAMUEL 15:10

Absalom is described in the Bible as very handsome, with no blemish in his appearance (2 Samuel 14:25)—but his heart appears to have been stained with treachery.

Absalom was David's third son, born to the daughter of the king of Geshur, located on the northeast border of Israel. Absalom first revealed his treacherous heart when his full sister Tamar was taken advantage of by Absalom's half brother Amnon, David's oldest son by another wife (2 Samuel 13). Absalom bided his time for two years without saying a word to Amnon, all the while, though, plotting his revenge. Absalom arranged for his men to kill Amnon during a sheep-shearing celebration—then he fled to his mother's home in Geshur.

Later Absalom was allowed to return to Jerusalem, and he and David were reconciled. Even then, however, Absalom was plotting more treachery—this time against his own father.

For four years, Absalom worked to gain favor with many people in Israel—then he staged an outright rebellion in Hebron, about twenty miles south of Jerusalem. David had to flee to Mahanaim on the other side of the Jordan River and even fought against Absalom's men. Eventually Absalom was killed, and the rebellion came to an end.

INFORMATION: Absalom may have staged his rebellion in Hebron because this was the town of his birth (2 Samuel 3:2–3). There were probably already people there who knew Absalom and would have been sympathetic to his desire to become king.

ABSALOM, King David's handsome son, who initiated a coup against his father, gets his long, beautiful locks caught in a tree branch during the rebellion, and is speared to death by soldiers loyal to the king. The image is from the floor of Italy's Cathedral of Siena.

# ADAM
## First Man

For it was Adam who was first created, and then Eve.
1 TIMOTHY 2:13 NASB

Adam knew both the privilege and the pain of being first. As the first person who ever lived, Adam had the honor of naming all the animals. He joyfully entered into the first marriage in a way that would be completely unique from every marriage that followed. He experienced an unparalleled relationship with God as he ate from the tree of life and walked with God in the Garden of Eden.

But Adam also experienced painful firsts. Together with his wife Eve, he was the first to disobey God, and his actions ushered sin into a perfect world. Sickness, death, pain, and a wealth of other difficulties came into not only the world but also his life as a result. While Adam knew the joy of welcoming the first baby into the world, he also knew the pain that came when that same son murdered his younger brother.

The Bible gives Adam a significant theological role by contrasting him directly with Christ. While sin and death entered the world through Adam, forgiveness and eternal life came through Jesus Christ. First Corinthians 15:22 says, "For as in Adam all die, so also in Christ shall all be made alive" (1 Corinthians 15:22 ESV). While humanity's allegiances were once aligned with Adam, Christians align themselves instead with Christ, who becomes the "author and perfecter of faith" (Hebrews 12:2 NASB).

INSIGHT: The theological importance of Adam (and his contrast in Christ) underscores the heart of the gospel message and Christian faith. Study more of the contrasts in Romans 5:12–21; 1 Corinthians 15:22, 45.

ADAM names the animals in the Garden of Eden. God had earlier declared, "It is not good for the man to be alone. I will make a helper suitable for him" (Genesis 2:18). When it becomes clear that the animals are not "suitable helpers," God creates Eve.

A Syrian archer's random shot finds the seam in King AHAB's armor, mortally wounding him. Dogs would lick up Ahab's blood—just as God's prophet Elijah predicted—when Ahab's chariot was washed down.

# AHAB
## King of Israel

And Ahab the son of Omri did evil in the sight of the LORD,
more than all who were before him.
1 KINGS 16:30 ESV

As Ahab's life shows, God's favor often has little to do with worldly success. By all worldly accounts, Ahab was a very successful leader. He ruled as king over Israel for twenty-two years (1 Kings 16:29), cementing his power through a shrewd political marriage to Jezebel, daughter of the king of Tyre. He was successful in several military campaigns and even persuaded the king of Judah to join him in his attempt to recover the city of Ramoth-gilead from the Arameans (1 Kings 22:3–4). Assyrian records recall how Ahab spearheaded a coalition of forces to fight against the Assyrians at Qarqar, and his own contribution of over half the chariots for the coalition demonstrates his great military strength in comparison to neighboring nations.

So does Ahab's great success reveal that God was pleased with him? Not at all. The Bible makes it clear that Ahab sinned more than all the kings of Israel before him (1 Kings 16:30), and God was greatly displeased with him. Ahab's marriage to Jezebel led him and his people to worship Baal and other idols, and his reign was marked by wickedness. In the end, the Lord ordained that Ahab would be killed by an archer as Israel fought against the Arameans to recover Ramoth-gilead, and his wife Jezebel would suffer a shameful death as well (2 Kings 9:30–37).

INSIGHT: 1 Samuel 16:7 makes it clear that "the Lord sees not as man sees: man looks on the outward appearance, but the Lord looks on the heart" (1 Samuel 16:7 ESV). It may have appeared to everyone else that Ahab was successful and enjoyed God's favor, but his heart was sold to wickedness, and God was not pleased with him. God is pleased when we humbly seek Him and turn from our wickedness, calling on Him to forgive us and change us to reflect His character (Micah 6:8; Romans 12:1).

# AHAZIAH
## King of Judah

Ahaziah was twenty-two years old when he became king, and he reigned in Jerusalem one year. His mother's name was Athaliah, a granddaughter of Omri king of Israel.

2 KINGS 8:26

As every parent knows, great danger lies in store for those who choose to walk in the company of the wicked (Psalm 1:1, 6). In Ahaziah's case, that danger eventually turned into awful reality.

To be fair, the deck seemed to be stacked against Ahaziah from the beginning, because he was born to Athaliah, who appears to have been the daughter of wicked King Ahab of Israel (2 Kings 8:26). By arranging for his daughter to marry King Jehoram of Judah, Ahab sealed a political alliance that gave him the upper hand between the two powers. As a result, the next few kings of Judah, including Jehoram's son Ahaziah, were forced to team up with the kings of Israel on various ventures.

As Ahaziah was visiting a wounded King Joram of Israel during one of those ventures (a battle at Ramoth-gilead), Jehu, an official in the army of Israel, killed both kings and then killed forty-two of Ahaziah's relatives who were coming to visit Joram (2 Kings 9–10). Ahaziah's reign was brought to an abrupt end after one year.

INFORMATION: Unfortunately, tragedy continued to plague Ahaziah's family even after Ahaziah died. Soon after his death, his power-hungry mother, Athaliah, tried to kill off the entire royal family, and she ruled Judah for six years. Only one of Ahaziah's sons, Joash, survived—thanks to the quick thinking of Ahaziah's sister Jehosheba. Eventually Ahaziah's son was crowned king, and Ahaziah's tragedies ceased (2 Kings 11).

# AMOS
## Shepherd and Prophet of Israel

Amos answered Amaziah, "I was neither a prophet nor the son of a prophet,
but I was a shepherd, and I also took care of sycamore-fig trees.
But the LORD took me from tending the flock and said to me,
'Go, prophesy to my people Israel.'"

AMOS 7:14–15

A common accusation in the world of American politics is that someone is a "Washington insider," meaning he (or she) is so well connected in the affairs of the federal government that he's not in touch or concerned with the affairs of the common voter. Instead, he is mostly concerned with using his position to benefit himself.

There were many such "Samaria insiders" among the prophets of Amos's day, but Amos was clearly not one of them. As Amos himself said, he was neither a professional prophet nor the son of a professional prophet, but rather, a simple shepherd and farmer of sycamore-fig trees (Amos 7:14–15). His chief qualification for prophesying to the kingdom of Israel was simply the Lord's calling on his life.

To be fair, though, Amos should not be caricatured as an uneducated country bumpkin who had a few spiritual jabs to give Israel. Instead, his prophecies reflect a deep understanding of God Himself and the world in which he lived. His prophecies must have emanated from a heart and mind that had been engaged in these two expansive thoughts throughout his simple life.

Amos's prophecies warned Israel of the coming of the great "Day of the Lord" that would bring judgment against the injustices of both the Israelites and their neighbors.

INSIGHT: Amos's special calling by God and his refusal to become absorbed into the self-serving world of the professional prophets challenge believers today to make sure they are continually being "salt and light" to the world (Matthew 5:13) and not simply becoming an indistinguishable part of it. At the same time, Amos's deep understanding of God and the world around him despite his simple vocation calls us to strive for the same, whatever our calling in life.

Elderly ANNA had long anticipated Israel's Messiah. When Mary and Joseph dedicated Jesus at the temple, Anna saw the Messiah with her own eyes.

# ANNA
## Prophetess and Widow
## Who Lived in the Temple

There was also a prophet, Anna. . . . She was very old; she had lived with
her husband seven years after her marriage, and then was a widow
until she was eighty-four. She never left the temple
but worshiped night and day, fasting and praying.

LUKE 2:36–37

It's almost too hard to imagine what that moment must have been like for Anna.
For probably sixty years she had been a widow living at the temple, worshipping
night and day, fasting and praying, even communicating prophecies to people.
No doubt many of her thoughts and prayers focused on the coming Messiah and
the redemption of Jerusalem.

Then all of a sudden, there He was—the Messiah—right in front of her.
She heard what godly Simeon had said about Him, about how this baby was the
Lord's salvation and a light to the Gentiles. Could it really be true?

Anna came up to Mary and Joseph, thanking God for them and for their
little baby, Jesus, the Savior of the world. What else could she say to them except
thanks to God? Anna had plenty to say later, though—to everyone she met who
was looking forward to the redemption of Jerusalem. She told them all about the
baby she had seen in the temple and the hope that He was bringing to the entire
world. Anna had seen the Messiah.

INFORMATION: Most scholars place Jesus' birth at about 5
BC, which means that Anna would have been about twenty-six years
old (and perhaps recently widowed) when the independent kingdom
of Israel under the Hasmoneans was overtaken by the vast Roman
Empire. Perhaps this is what led her to commit herself to fasting and
praying day and night in the temple for the rest of her life.

# APOLLOS
Christian Preacher and Coworker with Paul

[Apollos] began to speak boldly in the synagogue; but when Priscilla and Aquila heard him, they took him aside and explained the Way of God to him more accurately.
ACTS 18:26 NRSV

Everyone can use help understanding the gospel better. When Paul's coworkers Priscilla and Aquila first met Apollos at Ephesus, it was obvious that he was a very gifted teacher of the scriptures (Acts 18:24–25). But even he was lacking in certain aspects of his understanding about the gospel, and he needed Priscilla and Aquila's helpful correction to set him straight.

Apollos had all the credentials to be a key leader in the early church:

- He was well educated.
- He came from Alexandria, one of the most important centers of learning in the ancient world.
- He understood the Old Testament—and even Jesus—very well.
- He spoke about Jesus with great fervor.

With all these credentials, Apollos—and everyone around him—could have easily assumed that he didn't need help understanding God better. But when Priscilla and Aquila listened to his passionate preaching in the synagogue, they must have sensed that Apollos didn't have some things quite right. So they hospitably invited Apollos to their home and explained to him what was still missing in his understanding of the gospel.

Through Priscilla and Aquila's loving and insightful help, Apollos became an even greater preacher about Jesus. The Bible says that he traveled to Corinth and was a great help to the church (Acts 18:27). He even helped Paul in his ministry there (see 1 Corinthians 4:6).

INSIGHT: Never think that you or anyone else has ever fully "got it" with the good news about Jesus. From the newest believer to the most gifted preacher or Bible teacher, anyone can use help understanding Jesus better. Don't let pride keep you from learning more about God from others—and don't mistakenly think that someone else can be completely trusted to have it all figured out.

# ARAUNAH
## Sold a Threshing Floor to David

Araunah said to David, "Take it! Let my lord the king do whatever pleases him. Look, I will give the oxen for the burnt offerings, the threshing sledges for the wood, and the wheat for the grain offering. I will give all this."

1 CHRONICLES 21:23

The events that led to the sale of Araunah's threshing floor to King David were strange indeed—almost as unexpected as what God had in store next for Araunah's tract of land.

Araunah (some translations use the name Ornan in 1 Chronicles) was a Jebusite, one of the early inhabitants of Jerusalem before David took the city and made it his capital. Araunah owned a threshing floor on top of Mount Moriah. A threshing floor was simply a flat piece of compacted earth or stone where grain was separated from the inedible chaff that surrounds each kernel. Threshing was an essential step before the wheat harvest could be made into flour. Such floors were often located atop hills or high plains, where the winds could blow away the chaff, leaving behind the heavier kernels of grain.

David purchased Araunah's threshing floor after a devastating plague killed about seventy thousand Israelites. The plague was God's punishment for David's census, which had been conducted to determine how many fighting men he had at his disposal. A census was not wrong in itself—after all, God Himself had ordered the census recorded in the book of Numbers. But David's census seemed to be more about his own pride and self-assuredness than anything else. Toward the end of the plague, David came face-to-face with the angel of the Lord as he stood at Araunah's threshing floor. David begged for mercy, saying that he alone deserved the punishment—and the Lord relented. A prophet named Gad then instructed David to build an altar on the site. Araunah was happy to give David the land, along with the oxen, wood, and grain needed for the offerings. David, however, rebuffed Araunah's generosity and insisted on paying the full price, not wanting to offer sacrifices that cost him nothing.

Some years later, David's successor, Solomon, built the temple on the site of the old threshing floor.

INSIGHT: Araunah's former threshing floor was actually the perfect site for God's temple. Being situated on top of a hill gave the temple visual and strategic prominence amid the Jerusalem landscape.

# ASSYRIANS
## Nation That Exiled the People of Israel

In the ninth year of Hoshea, the king of Assyria captured Samaria and deported the Israelites to Assyria. He settled them in Halah, in Gozan on the Habor River and in the towns of the Medes.

2 KINGS 17:6

At their height of power, the Assyrians' military might was matched only by their cruelty and ruthlessness with their defeated foes.

The Assyrians lived in the northern part of what is known today as Iraq. They were the first nation to rule over the entire Fertile Crescent, stretching from the head of the Persian Gulf up to southeast Turkey and down into Palestine. For over three hundred years they pieced together their empire (911–612 BC), and at their height made major raids into Egypt.

As far as the people of Israel were concerned, the most significant event associated with the Assyrians was their attack at Samaria and the annexation of the northern kingdom of Israel in 722 BC. The Assyrians exiled many Israelites to faraway places and resettled other foreign peoples in Israel. As these foreign peoples intermarried with Israelites and combined their religious practices with the religion of Israel, they formed a group of people known as Samaritans. These people are spoken about later in several places in the New Testament (Matthew 10:5; Luke 17:16; John 4; Acts 8).

The Assyrian Empire was eventually overtaken by the Babylonians around 612 BC and later by the Persians.

INFORMATION: The Bible records another important event that occurred between the Assyrians and King Hezekiah of Judah: At one point, Hezekiah refused to pay the tribute that was expected of them by the Assyrians, so the Assyrians besieged Jerusalem. One night after Hezekiah prayed to the Lord, an angel went throughout the camp and killed 185,000 Assyrians. The king of Assyria withdrew to his own country, and Jerusalem was spared destruction (2 Kings 18–19).

# ATHALIAH
## Queue of Judah

Now when Athaliah the mother of Ahaziah saw that her son was dead,
she arose and destroyed all the royal family.
2 KINGS 11:1 ESV

At times it is simply astounding how pervasive the effects of one person's sin can be. From the alcoholic to the busybody to the self-indulgent, one person's sin can affect not only those around that person but also those who come after him or her. Athaliah is a sad demonstration of the pervasiveness of her father, Ahab's, sin.

Most Bible readers are already familiar with the wicked deeds of King Ahab of Israel (including his clashes with the prophet Elijah), but few realize that his sin continued even in the life of his daughter Athaliah. Athaliah married Jehoram, the oldest son of the godly king Jehoshaphat of Judah, and soon her wicked influence became visible. Jehoram "did evil in the eyes of the Lord," and the same was said of Ahaziah, the son born to him and Athaliah (2 Kings 8:18, 27). After Ahaziah was killed by Jehu (2 Kings 9:27), Athaliah saw her chance to seize the throne—and she attempted to kill off all the royal family of Judah. Only young Joash escaped as his aunt stole him away and hid him with a nurse in the temple for six years.

After six years of Athaliah's rule over Judah, a priest named Jehoiada staged a rebellion and brought out Joash to anoint him as king. Athaliah was killed, and the wicked influence of Ahab finally came to an end. The pervasive sin of Athaliah stands as a strong reminder to watch our own lives carefully for unchecked sinful attitudes or behaviors.

INTERESTING. . .Athaliah's wickedness (and that of her father, Ahab) extended even into the temple of the Lord, for at some point her sons "had broken into the temple of God and had used even its sacred objects for the Baals" (2 Chronicles 24:7).

The BABYLONIANS were a real power in their time, but—like all earthly powers—their time came and went while the power of God remained.

# BABYLONIANS
## Nation That Exiled the People of Judah

[The Lord] brought up against them the king of the Babylonians, who killed
their young men with the sword in the sanctuary, and did not spare
young men or young women, the elderly or the infirm. God gave
them all into the hands of Nebuchadnezzar.

2 CHRONICLES 36:17

As powerful as they were, ultimately the Babylonians functioned as a tool in the
hand of God. Unfortunately, God eventually needed to use that tool to bring
judgment on His people.

The Babylonians lived in the southern part of what is now known as Iraq,
between the Tigris and Euphrates rivers. They gained prominence under the
reign of Hammurabi, who united several smaller states and codified the laws of
the nation. Around 729 BC the Assyrians began to rule over them, but by 612
BC the Babylonians had joined with the Persians to break free from their grip
and take over much of their kingdom, including the regions of Israel and Judah.

Soon after this, the Babylonians became directly involved in Judean affairs
as different kings rebelled against them. The Babylonians under Nebuchadnezzar eventually attacked the capital city of Jerusalem in 586 BC, destroyed the city
and the temple, and exiled virtually all the leading citizens to Babylon.

By 539 BC, King Cyrus of Persia captured the city of Babylon and decreed
that all the Jews who had been exiled there could return to Judea.

INFORMATION: The capital of Babylonia was Babylon, which
was located about fifty-five miles south of modern-day Baghdad. The
walls of this city were immense, but Cyrus of Persia conquered the
city by diverting the flow of the Euphrates River, which ran under the
walls, thereby enabling his soldiers to enter the city.

BALAAM, unable to see the sword-wielding angel blocking his path, beats his donkey—which has turned away because it *does* see the angel.

# BALAAM
## Prophet with a Talking Donkey

And the donkey said to Balaam, "Am I not your donkey, on which you have
ridden all your life long to this day? Is it my habit to treat you this way?"
NUMBERS 22:30 ESV

The tale of Balaam and his talking donkey fascinates children, but his story carries a greater significance than what may be seen on the surface. When examined more deeply, the biblical narrative regarding Balaam ultimately points to the power and supremacy of God.

Biblical and archaeological history both confirm that Balaam was a renowned seer in the ancient world. When Balak, king of Moab, felt threatened by the Hebrews, he summoned Balaam. He hoped to hire Balaam to curse the Hebrews.

Even though Balaam was a spiritual person, there is no indication that he was a true prophet of God. He did, however, appear to know of God's power and feared Him enough to turn down Balak's initial request. When Balak persisted with offers of financial gain, Balaam agreed to meet him. (Read the entire story in Numbers 22–24.)

On Balaam's trek to Moab, God confronted the seer with profound reminders of His power: an angel with a flaming sword and a talking donkey (Numbers 22:27–28). With a stern rebuke and severe warning, God permitted Balaam to proceed on his journey. Arriving at his destination with God's admonition fresh in his mind, Balaam refused to curse the people of God but blessed them three times instead.

Balaam's story illustrates how the power of God trumps the evil intents of others. By using a talking donkey and a sinful seer, God showed that He can use anyone or anything to accomplish His plan—even unwilling or unusual participants.

INSIGHT: Balaam's story includes more than the episode involving
a talking donkey. Revelation 2:14 and Numbers 31:16 reveal that
Balaam instructed Balak to lead the Israelites into idolatry and sexual
sin. Balaam's story ended when he died in battle against the Israelites
as recorded in Numbers 31:16.

# BARABBAS
## Prisoner with Jesus

So Pilate, wishing to satisfy the crowd, released for them Barabbas,
and having scourged Jesus, he delivered him to be crucified.
MARK 15:15 ESV

To hear it makes our blood boil: a guilty man goes free, and an innocent man is condemned instead. For most of us, this will be the only association we ever have with the name Barabbas.

All we know about Barabbas himself is that he was a notorious prisoner who had been imprisoned for insurrection and murder some time before Jesus' arrest (Matthew 27:16; Mark 15:7; Luke 23:19; John 18:40). We don't know anything about the insurrection, nor do we know what happened to Barabbas after his release.

The only other thing we know about Barabbas is that this guilty man, for no reason other than the will of God carried out by Pontius Pilate, was released and set free, and Jesus, an innocent man, was condemned and executed instead. It all happened as part of Pilate's usual custom of releasing a prisoner chosen by the crowd during Passover (Matthew 27:15; Mark 15:6; John 18:39), and this time the religious leaders succeeded in stirring up the crowd to choose Barabbas instead of Jesus.

INSIGHT: It is completely right to be angry when we hear of such injustice being committed against Jesus, an innocent man. Yet if we reflect on our own salvation, every believer has stood precisely in Barabbas's place. We, being undeniably guilty in our sins, have been released from our death sentence for no reason of our own—it is simply by the gracious will of God—and Jesus has been condemned and executed in our place. From now on, when you hear the name Barabbas, praise God for the immeasurable grace He has shown every believer, and thank Him that you—though underserving—have been set free to serve Him.

# BARAK
## Military Leader of Israel

Barak said to [Deborah], "If you go with me, I will go;
but if you don't go with me, I won't go."

JUDGES 4:8

For better or worse, Barak was definitely not a lone ranger. When the Lord gave the prophetess Deborah a message for Barak and called him to fight the Canaanites under the command of Sisera, Barak basically said, "I'll do it if you will" (Judges 4:8). Deborah agreed to come but warned Barak that he would miss out on receiving glory for the victory.

So Barak and Deborah called up the forces of Israel, and they gathered at Mount Tabor on the edge of the great Jezreel Valley. Sisera soon mustered his men and led them—along with his nine hundred iron chariots—to the Kishon River to the south of the mountain, ready for battle. Barak and his men rushed down the mountain, sending Sisera's men fleeing for their lives. The Israelites pursued the Canaanites until there was no one left, and even Sisera himself was killed by a woman as he hid in her tent. After the battle was over, Barak and Deborah sang a victory duet, recounting the story of the great battle.

INFORMATION: Despite Deborah's warning to Barak, he did still receive some glory for defeating the Canaanites. The prophet/judge Samuel referred to Barak as being among those whom the Lord sent to deliver the Israelites from their enemies (1 Samuel 12:11). The author of the New Testament book of Hebrews also referred to Barak as being among those who are good examples of faith (Hebrews 11:32).

BARNABAS (with red robe) appeals to God while his coworker Paul (in gold robe) tries to stop the people of Lystra from sacrificing an ox to the Christian missionaries. After Barnabas and Paul had healed a lame man, the people concluded they were the gods Zeus and Hermes, respectively.

# BARNABAS
## Apostle and Coworker with Paul

Thus Joseph, who was also called by the apostles Barnabas
(which means son of encouragement), a Levite, a native of Cyprus. . .
ACTS 4:36 ESV

If people from your church gave you a nickname, what would it be? The Great
Helper? Miss Generous? Captain Gossip? We don't usually give people such
overtly suggestive nicknames, but people in Jesus' day did. One such nickname
for a leader in the early church was *Barnabas,* meaning "Son of Encouragement,"
and the nickname couldn't have been more fitting.

We first hear of Barnabas, whose given name was Joseph, during the early
days of the church. The Bible notes how at that time the believers were of one
mind, and no one was needy—because from time to time believers would sell
some possessions and bring the money to the leaders for distribution (Acts 4:32–
35). Barnabas is mentioned as being one of those generous people.

Later, Barnabas is mentioned again as the one who stood up for Paul (also
called Saul) before the other apostles in Jerusalem when Paul first became a believer (Acts 9:27). Barnabas also traveled to Tarsus, Paul's hometown, to ask him
to join in ministry at Antioch (Acts 11:25). Barnabas went with Paul on their
first missionary journey (Acts 13:1–3). At the outset of their second journey,
Barnabas was such a believer in people that he could not bear to exclude his relative Mark, who had abandoned them on the first journey, even though Paul was
insistent that Mark not be allowed to come (Acts 15:36–41).

INSIGHT: Barnabas's encouraging nature was so apparent to
everyone that they nicknamed him Son of Encouragement. Take a
moment to consider what your most recognizable traits are. Are you
seen as a person who encourages? Who helps? Who gives? Or would
others see you as someone who criticizes? Who avoids church work
days? Who is tight-fisted? Ask God to help you become a person who
is characterized by the fruit of the Spirit (Galatians 5:22–23).

BARTIMAEUS appears quite young in this statue in Hesse, Germany. The Bible doesn't specify Bartimaeus's age, but says that after his healing, he "followed Jesus."

# BARTIMAEUS
## Blind Beggar Who Saw Jesus

And Jesus said to him, "What do you want me to do for you?"
And the blind man said to him, "Rabbi, let me recover my sight."
And Jesus said to him, "Go your way; your faith has made you well."
And immediately he recovered his sight and followed him on the way.

MARK 10:51–52 ESV

We don't often see miracles happening at the corner coffee shop or outside our local courthouse building. But the crowds pressing through the city gates of Jericho certainly witnessed one as Jesus passed through their city one day long ago (Mark 10:46).

By the dusty roadside near the Jericho gate sat Bartimaeus, a blind man, begging from the ground among the jostling crowd. Suddenly, he heard a large crowd moving by and learned that Jesus of Nazareth was among them. Jesus! No more begging, he began shouting, "Jesus, Son of David, have mercy on me!" (Mark 10:47). The people around him reprimanded him for his noise, but he only shouted all the louder for the merciful Son of David.

Jesus must have heard his cry, for He stopped and told the crowd to call Bartimaeus to Him. Quickly, casting aside his cloak, Bartimaeus went to meet Jesus and told Him simply, "Rabbi, I want to see." Jesus replied, "Go, your faith has healed you" (Mark 10:51–52), and a healed, seeing Bartimaeus followed Him away from Jericho.

INSIGHT: Bartimaeus fervently called to Jesus because he recognized who Jesus was: the merciful Son of David. He was excited to be in the presence of the One who mercifully healed and worked in even the most seemingly impossible situations. Heal a blind person? Make him see? Bartimaeus had little doubt. He knew Jesus could heal him. What is our heart's attitude when we approach our Savior during difficult or traumatic times in life? Do we doubt His care, mercy, and ability to work for our good, or do we have the confidence of Bartimaeus when we call out, "Jesus, Son of David, have mercy on me"?

# BENAIAH
## Captain of David's Bodyguard

He [Benaiah] was held in greater honor than any of the Thirty, but he was not included among the Three. And David put him in charge of his bodyguard.
2 SAMUEL 23:23

Perhaps the most inspiring stories ever told revolve around others so completely devoted to something greater than themselves that they are willing to risk their very lives for it. Benaiah is a quintessential picture of such devotion.

Benaiah was from Kabzeel, a town in southern Judah, and he was the son of a man named Jehoiada. The only other information we know about Benaiah is about what he himself did. As one of David's bravest warriors, he killed two of Moab's best men. The story continues as he went down into a pit and killed a lion. Once he even disarmed a large Egyptian and killed him with his own weapon (2 Samuel 23:20–23)!

Probably as a reward for his bravery and wholehearted devotion, David put Benaiah in charge of his bodyguard, where Benaiah continued to demonstrate his loyalty to David. When Adonijah set himself up as king, Benaiah and his bodyguard unit were not invited to the coronation—probably because Adonijah knew that David had not authorized the event, and Benaiah would always side with David.

Benaiah's loyalty to David continued even under Solomon, whom David had appointed to be the next king. Benaiah faithfully and bravely carried out Solomon's orders to strike down Adonijah, Joab, and Shimei for their disloyalty to David, and he replaced Joab as the commander over the whole army.

INTERESTING. . . David's bodyguard was comprised of men from the Kerethites and Pelethites, who lived near the Philistines and may have been related to them. David may have gained their loyalty during the time that he sought refuge from Saul among the Philistines and lived at Ziklag.

# BEN-HADAD
## King of Aram

> Meanwhile, the officials of the king of Aram [Ben-Hadad] advised him, "Their gods are gods of the hills. That is why they were too strong for us. But if we fight them on the plains, surely we will be stronger than they."
>
> 1 KINGS 20:23

Theology matters. From Bible professors to the person sitting next to you on the bus, we all think certain things about God, and this will affect how we live and act. Unfortunately for King Ben-Hadad of Aram, he got his theology very wrong—and it led to a stunning defeat of his army.

There were several kings of Aram named Ben-Hadad, and all of them fought Israel at one time or another. The one who fought against King Ahab of Israel was Ben-Hadad II, likely the son of Ben-Hadad I.

Ben-Hadad mustered a vast coalition of forces and besieged Samaria, the capital city of Israel. He called for Ahab to surrender, but Ahab refused. Instead, he launched a preemptive attack that caught the drunken Arameans by surprise, and Ahab won a great victory.

Ben-Hadad's officers must have been looking for some excuse as to why they were unable to defeat Ahab's forces, so they offered a bit of bad theology to Ben-Hadad: The God of Israel is a god of the hills. Attack them on the plains, and you will win. They couldn't have been more wrong. When the Arameans attacked Israel again the next year, Ahab's forces defeated them again, killing one hundred thousand of them in a single day!

INSIGHT: The world is fond of portraying theology as a bunch of ivory-towered musings of the socially irrelevant elite. But in the end, how we think about God affects everything we do. Our beliefs about God will lead us either to our salvation or our demise. Don't be like Ben-Hadad—know the God of Israel and live.

# BERNICE
## Sister of King Agrippa II

Paul replied, "Short time or long—I pray to God that not only you but all who are listening to me today may become what I am, except for these chains." The king rose, and with him the governor and Bernice and those sitting with them.

ACTS 26:29-30

There is not enough room in the Bible to record everything about every person who encountered the gospel during Paul's ministry, but it's interesting to speculate about what some must have been thinking. For example, what was going on in the heart of Bernice when Paul was directly urging her to embrace the gospel?

Bernice was the daughter of Agrippa I, who was the grandson of Herod the Great, the king who reigned over Judea when Jesus was born. She was also the sister of Agrippa II.

Bernice had several short-lived marriages and eventually spent most of her time in the company of her brother Agrippa, which generated rumors of impropriety in their relationship. That was her situation when she encountered Paul at Caesarea.

Paul had been imprisoned at Caesarea because of a dispute with the Jewish leaders at Jerusalem. While he was there, Festus, the Roman governor, invited Agrippa and Bernice to hear Paul's case and help him decide what to do about Paul. Agrippa and Bernice arrived in great pomp, and Paul was allowed to speak. In the process, he boldly urged Agrippa and Bernice to become Christians! Agrippa and Bernice immediately left the room, declaring Paul to be innocent.

We hear nothing further about Bernice after this episode. Perhaps she was not moved at all by Paul's invitation. But perhaps she was. We can only hope.

INFORMATION: A few years after Paul's appeal to Agrippa and Bernice, the Jews revolted against the Romans, and the couple traveled to Jerusalem to appeal to the Romans to be merciful to the Jews. Their appeal was unsuccessful, and the Jews forced them to flee to Galilee, where they eventually gave themselves up to the Romans.

BERNICE observes the trial of the apostle Paul, as reported in Acts 25–26. The stained glass window is from St. Paul's Cathedral in Melbourne, Australia.

# BEZALEL
## Builder of the Tabernacle

"Bezalel and Oholiab and every craftsman in whom the Lord has put skill and intelligence to know how to do any work in the construction of the sanctuary shall work in accordance with all that the LORD has commanded."
EXODUS 36:1 ESV

Given the Bible's strong emphasis on godly living and faithfulness to the Lord, it might be tempting to think that such things as art and architecture are essentially secular, second-class concerns of God. The Lord's commission to Bezalel, however, proves this idea very wrong.

While Moses was on Mount Sinai, the Lord gave him very specific plans regarding how His people were to live and worship. Part of those plans included the construction of the tabernacle, essentially a mobile worship tent that housed the ark of the covenant and the altar. The Lord gave very specific instructions regarding how the tabernacle was to be built and how the priests were to dress and perform their duties. The Lord designated a man named Bezalel to head a team of artists to produce all the objects involved in worship. These people were skilled in working with gold, silver, bronze, stone, wood, and even fabric, and they were to use their skills to glorify God and lead others to glorify Him in worship. Their work would become a lasting part of the worship of God's people as they offered their sacrifices and prayers at the tabernacle generation after generation.

INSIGHT: Bezalel and those he trained were commissioned to a very noble calling, and they used their artistic skills to bring glory to God for generations to come. God continues to endow His people with gifts for the purpose of glorifying Himself and leading others to glorify Him as well (1 Corinthians 12; Romans 12). How might you use the gifts God has given you to glorify Him and lead others to do the same?

# BENJAMIN
## Brother of Joseph

As [Joseph] looked about and saw his brother Benjamin, his own mother's son,
he asked, "Is this your youngest brother, the one you told me about?"
And he said, "God be gracious to you, my son."

GENESIS 43:29

Some things never change. Brothers can fight among themselves like cats and dogs, but in the end, few other relationships are marked by greater loyalty and love than a brother for a brother. The relationship between Benjamin and Joseph may have been no different.

Benjamin was the younger brother of Joseph and the son of Rachel, the beloved wife of Jacob. Benjamin had eleven brothers in all, but only Joseph was his full brother. All the others were born to different mothers. Rachel died giving birth to Benjamin, and she wanted to name him Ben-Oni ("son of my sorrow"), but Jacob named him Benjamin ("son of my right hand/strength") instead (Genesis 35:18).

After Joseph had been sold into slavery by his brothers and had risen to a very high position within the Egyptian government, Joseph's brothers came to Egypt looking for food. They did not recognize Joseph when they saw him, but he recognized them. Joseph tested his brothers' hearts to see how they would respond, in the process blessing Benjamin much more than his brothers and showing his special love for the youngest. Eventually Joseph revealed his identity to the brothers and convinced them to move to Egypt with him. He continued to richly bless Benjamin with money and clothes (Genesis 45:22).

INFORMATION: Benjamin eventually became the father of a tribe of Israel by the same name, and these people were known as able warriors, many of whom were left-handed and able to sling a stone with great accuracy (Judges 20:15–16).

BOAZ talks with Ruth as she gleans in his field. The seventeenth-century painting is by the Dutch artist Nicolaes Pieterszoon Berchem.

# BOAZ
## Wealthy Bethlehemite Who Married Widowed Ruth

> Now Naomi had a relative on her husband's side, a man of standing
> from the clan of Elimelek, whose name was Boaz.
> RUTH 2:1

It is often in the smaller, less noticeable things we do that our true character is revealed. Do we impatiently stare at the checkout clerk working the long line ahead of us? Do we decide not to help with the new church ministry because we don't like the person in charge?

Surely Boaz faced similar decisions in his everyday life, but the Bible details various ways he showed unselfishness and concern for others—even at his own expense.

The book of Ruth recounts how Boaz, a farmer in Bethlehem, was a wealthy man, yet he took time to talk to others, such as his harvesters. He also took special notice of a young woman named Ruth who was gleaning in his fields, and he learned that she was the daughter-in-law of Naomi, the widow of his deceased relative Elimelek. Boaz made sure Ruth was protected and treated honorably while she gleaned in his fields. He provided her with abundant food and water and even instructed his men to purposely leave stalks of grain for her to gather.

Later Ruth appealed to Boaz that he marry her and purchase the land that had belonged to Naomi's husband so it would remain within the family. Boaz was certainly interested, but honorably and selflessly presented the offer first to a relative who was more closely related to Naomi. When the other relative declined, Boaz gladly acquired the land and Ruth as his wife.

Boaz and Ruth later had a son, Obed, who became an ancestor of David and ultimately an ancestor of Christ.

INFORMATION: By purchasing the land and marrying Ruth, Boaz acted in the Old Testament role of kinsman-redeemer. In ancient Israel, God's covenant with His people included the offer of a portion of the Promised Land as an inheritance, so it was critical that everything be done to prevent the loss of one's land. The kinsman-redeemer could help a struggling relative by purchasing his or her land to ensure that it remained with the family.

In a stained glass window from a French chapel, Jesus appears before CAIAPHAS.

# CAIAPHAS
## High Priest

But one of them, Caiaphas, who was high priest that year, said to them, "You know nothing at all. Nor do you understand that it is better for you that one man should die for the people, not that the whole nation should perish."
JOHN 11:49–50 ESV

Few things turn people's stomachs more than the abuse of power by religious leaders. Such people ought to be examples of godly, servant leadership—so when we see them clutching power and using it to serve themselves, we naturally feel angry and disgusted. Caiaphas certainly turned more than a few stomachs in his day, because it seems he was willing to do anything to retain his power.

Caiaphas was high priest and a member of the Jewish ruling council called the Sanhedrin. As Jesus grew in popularity and His miracles became well known, the religious leaders began to fear that the Romans would become involved. Caiaphas offered a simple solution: Kill Jesus so the rest of the nation—and no doubt his own power over it—wasn't destroyed. Caiaphas's solution eventually culminated in the crucifixion of Jesus (Matthew 26:3–4, 57; John 11:47–53).

Later, when Peter and John healed a crippled man at the temple, the religious leaders, including Caiaphas, became involved again. Peter boldly told the leaders that he and John had performed the miracle by the authority of Jesus Christ, whom the leaders had put to death. Even though the leaders recognized that their miracle was impossible to deny, they threatened Peter and John to keep them from talking about Jesus (Acts 3–4)!

INTERESTING. . . In 1990 twelve ossuaries—bone boxes—of the family tomb of a "Caiaphas" were discovered two miles south of Jerusalem. It is possible that this was the same Caiaphas as the one who plotted Jesus' death.

CAIN reacts in agony to God's judgment for the murder of Abel, saying, "My punishment is greater than I can bear." The marble statue is in St. Petersburg, Russia's, Hermitage Museum.

# CAIN
## Son of Adam and Eve

Cain said to his brother Abel, "Let us go out to the field." And when they were in the field, Cain rose up against his brother Abel, and killed him.
GENESIS 4:8 NRSV

Jealousy kills. And while Cain had intended only to kill his brother, the effects of his jealousy reached further than he could have imagined.

As the firstborn son of Adam and Eve, Cain became the third person to inhabit the earth. Together with his parents (and later his other brothers and sisters), Cain began to care for the earth and became a farmer (Genesis 4:2). But soon Cain—once the greatest achievement of Adam and Eve (Genesis 4:1)—became the scourge of his family when anger and jealousy drove him to murder his own brother. Not only did Cain's anger result in Abel's death, but it also brought painful consequences in his own life. God drove Cain away from his family to live as an outcast in the land of Nod. Cain's jealousy first destroyed his brother's life and the family's unity, and then it shattered his own life as well. First John 3:12 records, "We must not be like Cain who was from the evil one and murdered his brother. And why did he murder him? Because his own deeds were evil and his brother's righteous" (1 John 3:12 NRSV)

Although Cain showed no remorse for his crime, he still received God's gracious protection and was allowed to begin his own family and community in the land of Nod. Cain's sons and grandsons became the fathers of music, cattle keepers, and craftsmen who worked with bronze and iron (Genesis 4:22).

INTERESTING. . .The phrase, "Am I my brother's keeper?" originated with Cain. He said this to God after murdering his brother (Genesis 4:9).

# CLEOPAS
## Traveler to Emmaus with Jesus

One of them, named Cleopas, asked him, "Are you the only one visiting Jerusalem who does not know the things that have happened there in these days?"
LUKE 24:18

Have you ever imagined what it would be like to have Jesus Himself lead you through the scriptures, giving you a guided tour of all that the Bible says about Him? For a man in scripture simply known as Cleopas, that dream really came true.

On the very day that Jesus rose from the dead and the disciples found His tomb empty, Cleopas and another unnamed person were walking from Jerusalem to the small town of Emmaus about seven miles away. Along the way, Jesus came to them and began to talk with them as they walked—but they didn't recognize who He was. Jesus asked what they had been discussing, and they told Him about all that had happened to Jesus in Jerusalem—how some of the disciples had found the empty tomb, but that they had not seen Him yet.

Jesus recognized the doubt and uncertainty in their words, so He rebuked them for their slowness to believe God's words about Him through His prophets. Then He led them through the scriptures (the Old Testament at that time), showing them what was spoken about Him. When they reached Emmaus, Cleopas and his companion urged Jesus to share a meal with them. During the meal, they recognized Jesus, but He immediately disappeared! Right away they went and told the other disciples all that they had seen.

INSIGHT: Like Cleopas, when we are facing troubles and difficulties that we don't understand, we would do well to review and believe God's promises to us in the Bible. As we come to fully understand and accept those promises, we will find they provide us with abundant assurance that God loves us, that He is in control, and that He is continually working out His plans for us—plans for our good (Romans 8).

Many people discuss matters of theology around the dinner table. CLEOPAS and his friend, unknowingly, discussed the subject with Jesus.

# CORNELIUS
## God-Fearing Roman Centurion

At Caesarea there was a man named Cornelius, a centurion of what was known as the Italian Cohort, a devout man who feared God with all his household, gave alms generously to the people, and prayed continually to God.
ACTS 10:1-2 ESV

Cornelius has the distinction of being the first fully Gentile Christian recorded in scripture. Before Cornelius's conversion, Jews and even Samaritans (half-Jews who worshipped the Lord somewhat differently) had become Christians—but the Bible does not record that any Gentiles had become Christians yet, due in part to the fact that Peter and the other apostles did not even realize they could. But with Cornelius's conversion, all that would change forever.

Cornelius was a centurion—a Roman military officer—which would have normally put him at odds with Jews and perhaps many early Christians as well. But Cornelius had already demonstrated that God was at work in his life, because "he gave generously to those in need and prayed to God regularly" (Acts 10:2). One day God spoke to Cornelius and told him to send for the apostle Peter in another town about thirty miles away. Meanwhile, God was working in Peter's heart as well, showing him by a vision that all people—Gentiles as well as Jews—can find forgiveness of sins in Jesus Christ.

When Cornelius's men arrived at Peter's house, Peter went with them and shared the gospel with Cornelius's household. The Holy Spirit came upon the new believers, confirming that this was indeed a work of God.

INFORMATION: Though the Old Testament places a great deal of emphasis on the Jews as the chosen people of God (Genesis 12:1–3), there are still some passages that could have made it clear to Peter that God desires for Gentiles to follow Him as well. Jonah is corrected by God for his lack of concern for the wicked people of Nineveh even when they repented (Jonah 4). Psalm 87 also celebrates that various foreign peoples will be counted among those who know the Lord and registered as residents of Jerusalem.

# CRISPUS

## Synagogue Ruler in Corinth

Crispus, the synagogue leader, and his entire household believed in the Lord;
and many of the Corinthians who heard Paul believed and were baptized.

ACTS 18:8

At first glance, we may think that only Gentiles responded to Paul's preaching on his missionary journeys, but the Bible makes it clear that many Jews became believers as well. Crispus is a prime example.

Crispus was the ruler of the synagogue in Corinth, meaning he was the leading elder over the synagogue. After Paul preached the gospel at Athens, he traveled to Corinth, a very wealthy port city in southern Greece. Following his normal custom, Paul spent several weeks preaching in the synagogue, showing Jews that Jesus was the Messiah. Eventually, however, some of the Jews became angry and abusive toward Paul, leading him to direct his primary efforts toward the Gentiles. Despite the resistance of these Jews, however, Crispus and his entire household believed in Jesus and were baptized—and so did many other Corinthians, presumably including Jews from the synagogue (Acts 18:1–8).

Crispus and his household must have continued on in the faith, because Paul later made reference to him in 1 Corinthians (1 Corinthians 1:14).

INFORMATION: The city of Corinth had a long and distinguished history, and it was strategically located near the isthmus that connected southern Greece to the mainland. Every two years the Isthmian Games, similar to the Olympics, were held just outside the city. Partially due to the fact that it was a port city, Corinth had become renowned for its immorality, a problem that is reflected in the issues that Paul had to address later in the church.

DANIEL's accusers, who will be in his position tomorrow, will find the lions much more aggressive. "My God sent his angel," Daniel reported to King Darius, "and he shut the mouths of the lions" (Daniel 6:22 NIV).

# DANIEL
## Jewish Prophet and Royal Official of Babylon

Then the king placed Daniel in a high position and lavished many gifts on him.
He made him ruler over the entire province of Babylon
and placed him in charge of all its wise men.

DANIEL 2:48

Of all the people mentioned in scripture, few are spoken of as highly as Daniel.
Daniel probably came from the nobility of Judah, and he was a very young man
when he was taken into exile in Babylon. Despite his traumatic beginnings, however, Daniel prospered—both as an official in the Babylonian royal court and as
a follower of God.

Daniel first served in the court of Nebuchadnezzar along with his friends
Hananiah (Shadrach), Mishael (Meshach), and Azariah (Abednego), and quickly
distinguished himself by his great learning and understanding. Later Daniel interpreted various dreams for Nebuchadnezzar and was rewarded with promotions
and wealth. Daniel also interpreted a divine message given to Nebuchadnezzar's
son Belshazzar.

Daniel continued his distinguished government service even after the kingdom changed hands to the Persians. Yet his devotion to God remained unshaken,
as demonstrated by the fact that it was his regular times of prayer that were used
by his enemies to trap him. With God's help, Daniel survived the ordeal unscathed
and continued to prosper.

Daniel was also a prophet who received several visions from God, mostly
about the future rise and fall of various world powers.

INFORMATION: Daniel's fame as a righteous and wise person
must have been widely known even in his own day, because the prophet
Ezekiel, who also lived in Babylon during the exile, spoke of Daniel's
righteousness and wisdom three times in his book (Ezekiel 14:14, 20;
28:3).

# DAVID
## King of Israel

"But now your [Saul's] kingdom will not endure; the LORD has sought out a man after his own heart and appointed him ruler of his people, because you have not kept the LORD's command."
1 SAMUEL 13:14

Whether it's a eulogy at a funeral or a bit of reminiscing at the dinner table, it always seems like the best things are said about people when they are not around to hear it. In David's case, God's highest praise of him was spoken not to David but to Saul when the Lord was rebuking him for his unfaithfulness.

Understandably, David is famous for many things throughout his life—mostly good, but some bad. As a boy, he killed the giant Goliath and played the harp to soothe Saul's troubled spirit. Later he was forced to flee from Saul when Saul tried to kill him. After David assumed the throne of Israel, he fought a number of battles and established Israel as the dominant power in the region.

Still later, David committed adultery with Bathsheba and arranged for her husband's death. After he repented, David made preparations to build a new temple to replace the tent that housed the ark of the covenant, although it was actually his son Solomon who built the temple. All the while, David composed psalms expressing his love for God and calling on God to rescue him from his enemies.

So was God's highest praise of David about one of David's many accomplishments? Or about his skillful composition of praise songs? No. It was simply that David was "a man after [God's] own heart" (1 Samuel 13:14). That is what made David truly great in the eyes of God.

INSIGHT: As we strive to honor God in life, what should be our highest aspiration? That we accomplish great things for God? That we live a godly life? Certainly these are noble goals. But ultimately our chief concern should be that we seek to have a heart that reflects the heart of God. No other praise could be greater.

The boy DAVID returns home from battle with Goliath's head in one hand and the giant's sword in the other.

# DEBORAH
## Prophetess and Judge of Israel

And Deborah said to Barak, "Up! For this is the day in which the LORD has given Sisera into your hand. Does not the LORD go out before you?" So Barak went down from Mount Tabor with 10,000 men following him.
JUDGES 4:14 ESV

Deborah was a woman who knew what needed to be done and wasn't afraid to tell people. And apparently it was obvious to everyone else that she knew what she was talking about, because they listened.

We first read about Deborah, who was married to a man named Lappidoth, when she was leading the Israelites as a prophetess. She had set up her court in the hill country of Ephraim, roughly in the middle of the nation, and people came to her to have their disputes settled (Judges 4:4–5).

At some point, the Lord made it clear to Deborah that a man named Barak in the northern part of Israel was supposed to lead the Israelites to fight against the Canaanites who lived near him. When she told Barak, he must have gotten cold feet—but he trusted Deborah, because he refused to go into battle unless she went with him (Judges 4:7–8). Deborah agreed to go, but she warned Barak that, as a result, he would forfeit the glory for the victory. In the end, Deborah and Barak won a great victory over the Canaanites, and they celebrated by singing a victory song together.

INTERESTING. . . The hill country of Ephraim, where Deborah set up her court, was home to several other early leaders of Israel. The judge Ehud lived there (Judges 3), as did the judge/prophet Samuel (1 Samuel 7:15–17) and the first king, Saul (1 Samuel 9:1–4).

DEBORAH was a judge in both senses of the word—one who addressed legal issues and a military deliverer.

# DEMAS
Coworker of Paul

For Demas, in love with this present world, has deserted me and gone to Thessalonica. Crescens has gone to Galatia, Titus to Dalmatia.
2 TIMOTHY 4:10 ESV

It's interesting how various people in the Bible have become forever identified by a single event in their lives. Enoch walked with God and was taken away, perhaps meaning he never died. Jabez prayed for God's blessing and deliverance from harm, and God granted his request. Judas betrayed Jesus to death with a kiss for thirty pieces of silver. Unfortunately for Demas, the echo that continues to ring from his brief mention in scripture is his desertion of Paul during his time of great need.

Scripture does not include much about Demas, but we can infer some general impressions from what is included. In his letters to the Colossians and to Philemon (Colossians 4:10; Philemon 24), Paul mentions Demas in positive words and in very good company, along with Mark (Barnabas's relative), Luke (the doctor and Gospel writer), and Aristarchus (Paul's coworker and fellow prisoner). Paul's words give us every reason to believe that at that time Demas was his trusted, faithful coworker.

The only other mention of Demas occurs several years later as Paul, facing the possibility of martyrdom, asks Timothy and Mark to come to him. Paul notes that only Luke is with him, because two other coworkers have gone elsewhere, while Demas, out of love for this world, has deserted him. We never hear anything more of Demas—whether he ever returned to serve the Lord or whether he continued on his selfish path to his own destruction, we don't know. In any event, those final, sad words have largely defined Demas through history.

INSIGHT: Demas may indeed have returned to the Lord—or he may have continued in his sin. Either way, his life stands as an example of the constant need to guard against sin. If even faithful, trusted coworkers of Paul could eventually fall prey to selfish, sinful desires that lead them away from God, how much more can believers today?

# DOEG
## Saul's Edomite Servant

The king [Saul] then ordered Doeg, "You turn and strike down the priests."
So Doeg the Edomite turned and struck them down. That day he killed
eighty-five men who wore the linen ephod.

1 SAMUEL 22:18

Loyalty is normally an admirable trait, but not if it means devotedly carrying out the wicked orders of a man gone mad with jealousy. But such was the twisted character of Doeg the Edomite, King Saul's head shepherd.

Soon after David had been anointed to be the next king and grew in popularity, Saul grew jealous and began to threaten David's life. David fled, stopping first at Nob, where many of the priests and their families lived. A priest named Ahimelek gave David and his men some of the sacred bread that was there, as well as the sword of Goliath. Doeg the Edomite happened to be there and saw David and his men.

Later, when Saul was accusing his officials of conspiring with David, Doeg stepped forward and volunteered the information he had about David and his men stopping at Nob. So Saul and his men went to Nob, but Ahimelek denied that he was guilty of any wrong. When Saul ordered his men to kill all the priests, his men refused—so Saul gave the order to Doeg, who murdered eighty-five priests and their families (1 Samuel 21–22).

INFORMATION: We can only speculate why Doeg was willing to betray David and to kill eighty-five priests and their families. Perhaps he saw it as his chance to gain favor with the king and rise above his lowly role as head shepherd. It is also possible Doeg's heritage as an Edomite fostered a hatred of Israelites in general, because Saul had fought against the Edomites earlier in his reign as king of Israel (1 Samuel 14:47).

# DORCAS
## Disciple Whom Peter Raised from the Dead

In Joppa there was a disciple named Tabitha (in Greek her name is Dorcas); she was always doing good and helping the poor.
ACTS 9:36

Dorcas was a continual witness to the power of God at work in her life, from her generosity with her possessions, to her own labors of love, to her amazing experience of being raised to life again by Peter.

Dorcas, also known as Tabitha, lived in the town of Joppa, one of the few port cities of Israel. The Bible describes her as a disciple who was known and loved as a very generous woman toward the poor. She made clothing for others and was always doing good.

While Peter was ministering in the city of Lydda nearby, Dorcas became sick and died—and some believers brought Peter to see what had happened. When he arrived, some widows were mourning her death and showed Peter some clothes that Dorcas had made for them.

Peter sent everyone from the room and prayed to God. Then he turned to Dorcas, telling her to get up—and she did! News of this amazing miracle spread throughout Joppa, and many people believed in the Lord.

INFORMATION: Dorcas's generous gifts of clothing for others are made even more admirable when we realize that clothing was typically much more expensive in ancient times than it is today. The making of cloth and clothing was essentially an entirely manual process, so it took a long time to make a single item. As a result, clothing was expensive, and people could not usually afford many sets of clothing.

DORCAS rises from the dead, in a painting found in a Roman basilica. When Peter brought the woman back to life, according to the Bible account, there was no one else in the room.

PLACIDO COSTANZI
FECE 1737

# EDOMITES
## Descendants of Esau and Neighbor of Israel

This is the account of the family line of Esau the father
of the Edomites in the hill country of Seir.
GENESIS 36:9

Though the Edomites were closely related to the Israelites, it seems that when the Israelites needed their help the most, the Edomites did more harm than good.

The Edomites were the descendants of Esau, who was the son of Isaac and the twin brother of Jacob (Genesis 32:3). The Edomites settled in the mountainous region to the southeast of Israel (which was called Canaan at the time), driving out the Horites who were there (Genesis 36:9).

The shaky relationship between Israel and Edom becomes evident very early, when the Israelites were seeking permission from the Edomites to pass through their territory on their way to the Promised Land of Canaan. The Edomites denied them permission to pass through and threatened to attack the Israelites if they tried to do so (Numbers 20).

Years later, Saul and David fought against the Edomites, and David eventually brought them under the rule of Israel (1 Samuel 14:47; 2 Samuel 8:11–14). After Israel split into two kingdoms, the Edomites remained under the rule of Judah for a time and even helped King Jehoshaphat of Judah fight against Moab (2 Kings 3). But later the Edomites regained their independence during the reign of King Jehoram of Judah (2 Kings 8:20–22).

When the Babylonians attacked Judah in 586 BC, the Edomites displayed disloyalty to their relatives again. Instead of helping them, it seems that they capitalized on Judah's weakened state and made raids on them as well (Obadiah 1–21).

By the time the Jews returned from exile in Babylon, many Edomites had moved into southern Judah, and it became known as Idumea.

INFORMATION: At the time when Jesus was born, Herod the Great was king of Judea, but he was not even fully an Israelite. He was an Idumean.

# EHUD
## Left-Handed Judge of Israel

Then the people of Israel cried out to the LORD, and the LORD raised up for them a deliverer, Ehud, the son of Gera, the Benjaminite, a left-handed man. The people of Israel sent tribute by him to Eglon the king of Moab.

JUDGES 3:15 ESV

Throughout history, people have associated left-handedness with all sorts of things, both good and bad: natural artistic talent, clumsiness, even misfortune. For Ehud, however, left-handedness put him at a great advantage for striking a crippling blow to the Moabites who were oppressing Israel during his time.

Ehud came from the tribe of Benjamin, who apparently were renowned in Israel for their many left-handed warriors (Judges 20:16; 1 Chronicles 12:2). The Moabites, however, were no doubt unaware of this tribe's distinctive warriors, and this ultimately led to their defeat.

King Eglon of Moab had attacked Israel and taken over the city of Jericho, called the City of Palms. Ehud was chosen to take the Israelites' tribute money to Eglon at Jericho. But Ehud brought another surprise for Eglon. Being left-handed, Ehud strapped a small sword to his right thigh. Since most people would have been right-handed and reached for their swords on their left thigh, Ehud's sword must have gone unnoticed by the Moabite guards, who would likely have been checking his left thigh for any weapons.

After being granted access to the king to hand over the tribute money, Ehud drew his sword, killed Eglon, and escaped back to Israel to call his fellow Israelites to arms. The Israelites seized control of Jericho and even made Moab subject to them. Ehud continued to serve Israel as judge for the rest of his life.

INFORMATION: Jericho is one of the oldest known cities in the world, dating back several thousand years. Even though Ehud lived probably no more than a few hundred years after Israel entered the Promised Land of Canaan, Jericho would have already been a very old, established city.

ELI, in happier times, telling the infertile Hannah that she will indeed bear a son. The boy, Samuel, will ultimately succeed Eli as priest of Israel.

# ELI
## Priest of Israel

Now the young man Samuel was ministering to the LORD in the presence of Eli. And the word of the LORD was rare in those days; there was no frequent vision.

1 SAMUEL 3:1 ESV

It's a classic model: An enthusiastic visionary founds an organization and steers it to excellence, but over time the organization is drained dry as less dedicated leadership allows things to grow more and more lax. That must have been the general tenor of things by the time Eli's priestly ministry in Shiloh was winding down.

Eli himself is not necessarily spoken of in scripture as corrupt or sinful, but it appears that he had let his own sons, who also served as priests, become very corrupt and abusive of their office (1 Samuel 2:10–18). Because of this, Eli's family was cursed by God—and this may be the reason that few people received special messages or visions from the Lord (1 Samuel 2:27–36).

In the meantime, God was raising up Samuel to replace Eli's sons as priests and leaders of the people. Samuel had been brought to Shiloh as a young boy and left in the care of Eli (1 Samuel 2–3). The final blow to Eli's family came when the Israelites were fighting against the Philistines. Both of Eli's sons were killed as they carried the ark of the covenant into battle, and even Eli himself fell over backward and broke his neck when he heard the news that the ark had been captured (1 Samuel 4).

INSIGHT: It is very shortsighted to think that all we need to concern ourselves with is our own spiritual walk. But this attitude leaves the spiritual lives of those who come after us in jeopardy. What are we doing to promote faithfulness to God in the lives of our children and others entrusted to our care?

A depiction, by Ilya Repin, of Job being encouraged or criticized his friends. The young man sitting quietly behind Job may be ELIHU.

# ELIHU
## Friend of Job

Now Elihu had waited before speaking to Job because they were
older than he. But when he saw that the three men
had nothing more to say, his anger was aroused.

JOB 32:4-5

Elihu in the book of Job is a bit of an enigma. He seems to come out of nowhere,
ready to set things straight with both Job and Job's friends, yet in the end, he, too,
seems to fall short of truly addressing Job's concerns.

We don't hear about Elihu until the last several chapters of Job (Job 32–37).
By this point in the story, Job has experienced great suffering, the reasons for
which are not at all clear to him, for he was a righteous man. Three of Job's
friends have come to visit him and then begin to offer various reasons why Job
must be experiencing suffering. For the most part, their reasons boil down to a
basic belief that all suffering is the result of sin on the part of the sufferer, so Job
must have sinned in some way.

Finally, with no previous mention of his existence in the story, Elihu speaks.
He begins by saying that he was waiting to speak because he is younger than the
other friends, but he has become frustrated by their failure to adequately explain
the reason for Job's troubles. Then he begins his monologue, mostly saying that
there is a disciplinary role in suffering and that this should be accepted. But even
if Elihu's words are true, why would Job, a righteous man, be disciplined by God?

Eventually Elihu's words are cut off by the Lord (Job 38:1), who speaks
from the storm to address Job, and this brings all disputing to a close.

INFORMATION: Elihu is described as a Buzite, which may
mean that he was descended from Nahor, Abraham's brother (Genesis
22:20–21). The descendants of Buz appear to have lived somewhere
in the desert of Arabia near the desert oases of Tema and Dedan
(Jeremiah 25:23–24).

The prophet ELISHA refuses the gifts of Naaman, whom he had just healed. His hand is on an open book, perhaps symbolizing his reliance on the word (and provision) of God.

# ELISHA
## Prophet of Israel and Successor of Elijah

And Elisha prayed, "Open his eyes, LORD, so that he may see." Then the LORD opened the servant's eyes, and he looked and saw the hills full of horses and chariots of fire all around Elisha.

2 KINGS 6:17

Throughout his entire ministry, Elisha was a man acutely aware of God's presence and power. He never lacked confidence in God's watchful care of him, and he seemed to call upon God's power as naturally as he carried out all his other tasks.

Perhaps this confidence was a result of witnessing firsthand all the ways that God watched over his mentor, Elijah, through even the most threatening of situations. Elijah had promised that if Elisha saw him taken up to heaven in a fiery chariot, he would receive a double portion of the spirit that rested on Elijah. Elisha did indeed see this, and the truth of this promise is evidenced by the fact that he performed twice as many miracles as Elijah.

Some of the miracles that Elisha took part in included curing the salty water of Jericho, witnessing Israel's miraculous victory over Moab, providing oil (and later a son) for a Shunammite woman, raising the Shunammite woman's son from the dead, curing some poisonous stew, healing Naaman's leprosy, causing an axhead to float in water, predicting that the Arameans would give up their siege of Samaria, and foretelling King Jehoash's victories over the king of Aram.

INTERESTING. . . The power that rested on Elisha apparently continued even after his death. One time when a few Israelites were burying someone, they threw the body into Elisha's tomb to escape a band of Moabite raiders. When the body touched Elisha's bones, the man came to life again (2 Kings 13:21)!

# ELKANAH
## Husband of Hannah

Whenever the day came for Elkanah to sacrifice, he would give portions
of the meat to his wife Peninnah and to all her sons and daughters.
But to Hannah he gave a double portion because he loved her,
and the Lord had closed her womb.

1 SAMUEL 1:4-5

Elkanah plays a relatively minor role in the story of Hannah and Samuel, but
even so, he serves as a positive example of godly love that goes against the grain
of culture.

Elkanah was the husband of two wives, Hannah and Peninnah. Peninnah
had children, but Hannah did not, and this was a source of great tension between
the two wives. In the culture of Bible times, one of the most important roles a
woman could fulfill was to bear children for her husband. If she was unable to do
that, she was often despised or ignored by her husband and treated disdainfully
by other women. In fact, Peninnah would often provoke Hannah because of this
and cause her to become very sad and upset whenever they went up to worship
at the tabernacle at Shiloh.

Elkanah, however, demonstrated godliness by showing true love for his wife
Hannah. When they would offer sacrifices and then prepare to eat the meal as
part of the sacrifice, Elkanah would give Hannah a double portion of food as a
demonstration of his care for her even while she was unable to bear children.

Later the Lord blessed Hannah and Elkanah and allowed Hannah to become pregnant. She eventually gave birth to the great prophet Samuel.

INFORMATION: The priest who presided over the tabernacle
during Elkanah's time was Eli, who gave a blessing to Hannah that she
might be able to conceive. Years later, Samuel would be raised by Eli in
the tabernacle, and he would even replace him as priest.

# ELYMAS
## Jewish Sorcerer Blinded by Paul

But Elymas the magician (for that is the meaning of his name) opposed them,
seeking to turn the proconsul away from the faith.

ACTS 13:8 ESV

The short story of Elymas (also called Bar-Jesus), which takes up a mere seven
verses of scripture (Acts 13:6–12), is filled with contrasts from start to finish.

Paul and Barnabas encountered Elymas at Paphos after traveling through
the island of Cyprus. Elymas, a Jewish sorcerer and false prophet, was an attendant of the Roman proconsul in Paphos. As Paul and Barnabas tried to share the
truth of the Gospel with the proconsul, Elymas tried to turn him from the faith.
So Paul rebuked Elymas and told him that the Lord was going to blind him for a
time, which is exactly what happened. After that, the proconsul was amazed and
believed in the Lord.

Three stark contrasts stand out in the story: First, as a Jew, Elymas was supposed to worship the Lord and refrain from practicing divination and sorcery
(Leviticus 19:26; Deuteronomy 18:10–13; Ezekiel 13:9, 20; Micah 3:6–7), yet
he was doing these very things in the service of the Roman proconsul. Second,
Elymas was characterized by deceit and trickery (Acts 18:10), yet he wanted
to turn the proconsul from the truth of the Gospel. And third, Elymas was no
doubt employed by the proconsul, because he offered special knowledge and
power through sorcery—yet in the end Elymas himself was blinded and needed
to be led by the hand.

INFORMATION: Elymas is described in the Bible as a
"sorcerer," which is actually the Greek word *magos*. This is the same
word (plural, magi) used for the "wise men" who came from the East,
probably Persia or Babylonia, to worship the young Jesus (Matthew
2:1–2). By Roman times, magi had become associated with magic and
divination, and many of them had flocked to the Roman Empire to
profit from their practices.

# ENOCH
## Man Who Walked with God

Enoch walked with God; and he was not, for God took him.
GENESIS 5:24 NASB

There are some things in the Bible we will likely never fully understand until we get to eternity. The single, simple, yet puzzling statement in Genesis 5:24 regarding Enoch's experience with God is undoubtedly one of them.

What does it mean that Enoch "walked with God"? What does it mean that God "took him" away? Scholars and laypersons alike have pondered the exact meaning of these words for thousands of years, but no one knows for sure. Most believe that "walked with God" means that he lived a godly life in close communion with God. As a result, Enoch was translated straight to heaven without experiencing death (see Hebrews 11:5).

Besides genealogies, the only other places Enoch is mentioned in the Bible are Hebrews 11:5, where he is commended as a man of faith who pleased God, and Jude 14, where he is said to have prophesied regarding the Lord's return.

Are you interested in growing in your spiritual life? Spend time contemplating what it might have meant for Enoch to "walk with God"—and incorporate some of those traits into your own life.

INFORMATION: Beginning a few hundred years before the birth of Jesus Christ, several works were written as prophecies of Enoch. Some of these were included in certain versions of the Bible, such as the Ethiopic Bible and the Old Slavonic Bible. It is likely that one of these books, commonly called 1 Enoch, is the one referred to by Jude (though this does not imply that 1 Enoch is inspired scripture), and the books of 1 Peter and Revelation may draw imagery from this book as well.

The Bible doesn't say exactly how God "took" ENOCH. . .but this illustration from an early eighteenth-century book shows him rising on a cloud in front of several witnesses.

# EPAPHRODITUS
## Coworker of Paul

I have thought it necessary to send to you Epaphroditus my brother and fellow worker and fellow soldier, and your messenger and minister to my need.
PHILIPPIANS 2:25 ESV

"A friend in need is a friend indeed." This is certainly true regarding Epaphroditus's faithful service to Paul. While Paul was in prison for preaching the gospel, the church in Philippi sent Epaphroditus to him with a gift to help provide for his needs. Epaphroditus faithfully delivered the gift to Paul, but he also became very ill—perhaps from the long journey—and almost died. Epaphroditus recovered, however, and Paul planned to send him back to the Philippians so that they no longer needed to be concerned for Epaphroditus's health.

Paul commended Epaphroditus to them as a "almost died for the work of Christ. He risked his life to make up for the help you yourselves could not give me" (Philippians 2:25, 30). He even encouraged the Philippians to "hold men like him in high regard" (Philippians 2:29).

INFORMATION: Philippi was the first city in Europe where Paul planted a church. On the Sabbath, he went to a nearby river to find a place of prayer, and he began to share the gospel with some women who had gathered there. One of the women who responded in faith was Lydia from the city of Thyatira in Asia Minor (Acts 16:12–14). Given his warm words in his letter to the Philippians, Paul must have always had very favorable regard for the church in Philippi, and their gift to him while he was in prison reflects that the feeling must have been mutual.

# EPHRAIM
## Son of Joseph and Father of a Half-Tribe of Israel

He blessed them that day and said, "In your name will Israel pronounce
this blessing: 'May God make you like Ephraim and Manasseh.'"
So he put Ephraim ahead of Manasseh.

GENESIS 48:20

From Joseph to David to many of the first Christians, one of the key themes that
is repeated throughout the Bible is God's favor being shown to those who are
regarded by the world as less important. Ephraim is yet another example of this
wonderful habit of God.

Ephraim was born the younger son of Joseph, who had been sold into slavery in Egypt by his older brothers. By the providence of God, Joseph rose to a
very high position in the Egyptian kingdom, and Pharaoh gave him a wife from
among the Egyptian priestly classes. This wife bore him two sons, Manasseh and
Ephraim.

When the time came for Joseph's father, Jacob, to bless his grandsons, Joseph brought the boys to him and placed Manasseh, who was the firstborn, at
Jacob's right hand, expecting him to receive the greater blessing. But Jacob chose
instead to give the greater blessing to Ephraim, the younger. No reason is given
for why he chose to do this; he simply did it.

Eventually Ephraim's descendants would become one of the most prominent tribes of Israel, and the northern kingdom would even be referred to at
times as Ephraim.

INSIGHT: In the thinking of the world, it is those who demonstrate
themselves as especially deserving who should receive special honor
or blessing from God or others. But that is not God's way. In God's
kingdom, the first are last, and the last are first (Matthew 20:16). God
chooses to bless us simply because of His good pleasure and grace, not
because of anything we have done (Romans 9:15–16; Ephesians 2:8–9).

The king wanted his wives to be beautiful—so much so that ESTHER was given a year of beauty treatments before entering his presence. But Esther had more going for her than just beauty. She was smart, courageous, considerate, and loyal, as well.

# ESTHER
## Queen of Persia

"For if you [Esther] remain silent at this time, relief and deliverance for the Jews will arise from another place, but you and your father's family will perish. And who knows but that you have come to your royal position for such a time as this?"
ESTHER 4:14

Whether it's a fan catching a home run baseball in the World Series or a parent catching her child as she falls off a swing set, so much of life is about being at the right place at the right time. Queen Esther seemed to be at the right place and the right time to save her people, the Jews. Would she risk her life to try?

Esther was a Jew living in the mighty Persian Empire, which stretched from the borders of India to the edges of Europe. Many years earlier, Jews had been exiled from their homeland of Israel and scattered throughout places that would eventually be engulfed by the Persian Empire. Esther had been chosen by the king of Persia as his new queen, but she was still only allowed to come into his presence if it pleased him to do so.

When wicked Haman, a high official in the Persian Empire, devised a plan to eradicate all Jews, Esther's relative urged her to take advantage of her privileged position in the empire to save her people. At the risk of her life, she approached the king and invited him to a banquet, where she revealed Haman's plot. The king executed Haman and saved the Jews by allowing them to defend themselves against those who tried to carry out Haman's plan.

INSIGHT: We'll probably never be faced with saving God's people from total eradication—but we all encounter situations where we are placed in the right place at the right time to do something for God. Whether it is giving part of a bonus to missions or spending a free evening helping out with a church youth group event, look for opportunities to make a lasting impact on God's kingdom with the resources you have been given.

Philip makes the most of an enquiring mind and brings THE ETHIOPIAN EUNUCH to Christ.

# THE ETHIOPIAN EUNUCH
## Official Met by Philip

So he [Philip] started out, and on his way he met an Ethiopian eunuch, an important official in charge of all the treasury of the Kandake (which means "queen of the Ethiopians"). This man had gone to Jerusalem to worship.

ACTS 8:27

Once in a great while it happens. Someone begins asking us questions about God or the gospel, and before we know it, he or she has virtually rolled out the red carpet to be led to Christ. That's the situation with the Ethiopian eunuch whom Philip encountered on the road to Gaza.

Ethiopia was the same country that was called Cush in the Old Testament. It was located south of Egypt in Africa, hundreds of miles from Israel. During the time of the Babylonian conquest of Judah, many Jews fled to Ethiopia to escape. Their influence may have been what led to a large following of native Ethiopians to worship the God of Israel.

By the time of the New Testament, Ethiopia had been ruled by several queens, all taking the title Kandake, or Candace—much like the title Caesar of the Roman Empire. The eunuch was an official of this kingdom, and he had just been to Jerusalem to worship there. The Lord led a Christian leader named Philip to go down to Gaza, where he met the eunuch reading the scriptures in his chariot. As they began to talk, the eunuch asked Philip to explain who was being talked about in Isaiah 53—and Philip told him that this referred to Jesus. The eunuch became a believer, and then he was baptized. Philip was then led by the Spirit to Azotus, and the eunuch went on his way rejoicing (Acts 8:26–40).

INTERESTING. . . Though it is only speculation, it is possible that the Ethiopian eunuch was actually looking for a passage in Isaiah 56:3–4, and he may have only unrolled the scroll as far as chapter 53 by the time Philip met him.

EVE, in a seventeenth-century painting by Hendrik Goltzius, holds the forbidden fruit, portrayed as an apple. The Bible never says exactly what the fruit was.

# EVE
## The First Woman and Mother of All People

When the woman saw that the fruit of the tree was good for food and pleasing to the eye, and also desirable for gaining wisdom, she took some and ate it. She also gave some to her husband, who was with her, and he ate it.

GENESIS 3:6

It's sobering to realize that a lifetime of good can be forever marred by a single sin or poor decision, and the consequences can be seemingly immeasurable. In the case of Eve, the consequences of her sin affected the entire world for the rest of time.

As most people know, Eve was the first woman, created by God from a rib from Adam's side. She and Adam lived in a beautiful garden in perfect harmony with God and with the rest of creation—until she and Adam chose to disobey and eat from the one tree that they were forbidden to eat from in all the garden.

Certainly when Eve ate the fruit, she never imagined all the harm that her sin would cause. Yet that is the nature of sin. It looks pleasing and harmless, but the final result is always death. No amount of blaming each other or the serpent, who tempted her to eat the fruit, could change the sad consequences that would forever plague Adam and Eve and all their descendants. Forced to leave the garden, their lives—and the lives of all who have come after them—would now be marked by hard work, pain, and sorrow.

INFORMATION: After Adam and Eve were forced to leave the garden, Eve gave birth to Cain and Abel. Years later, Cain killed Abel out of jealousy, but God gave Eve another son named Seth. Eve likely had other sons and daughters as well (Genesis 5:4).

EZRA gets back to basics, reading the book of the Law to the exiles returning to Jerusalem.

# EZRA
## Priest and Scribe after the Exile

For Ezra had devoted himself to the study and observance of the Law
of the LORD, and to teaching its decrees and laws in Israel.
EZRA 7:10

Ezra was a man with a very clear sense of purpose for his life: He had devoted himself to the study and observance of God's laws and to teaching them to God's people.

Ezra was both a priest and a scribe. As a priest, he was trained in the rituals and laws regarding atonement for sin and coming before God on behalf of the people. As a scribe, Ezra's chief goal was to preserve and pass on the scriptures and explain them to others. Ezra led a group of about five thousand Jewish exiles from Babylon to Judea around 459 BC, about seventy years after the first waves of exiles were allowed to return. The dangerous journey took about four months.

After Ezra arrived in Judea, he immediately began addressing wrongs that were being done in the land, and he led the people in repentance and recommitment to follow God's laws (Ezra 9–10). Soon after the walls of Jerusalem were rebuilt, Ezra read the law from morning until midday, and this sparked a new fervor among the people to follow God's laws (Nehemiah 8).

Jewish tradition also holds that Ezra founded the Great Assembly, which was the forerunner of the Sanhedrin, the council of Jewish leaders.

INTERESTING. . . The book of Ezra, which may have been written by Ezra himself, is one of two books in the Bible that has significant portions of it written in Aramaic, a sister language to Hebrew. The other is the book of Daniel, which was also written around the time of the exile. Aramaic was the language of the Babylonian Empire.

# FESTUS
## Governor of Judea

When two years had elapsed, Felix was succeeded by Porcius Festus.
And desiring to do the Jews a favor, Felix left Paul in prison.
ACTS 24:27 ESV

Festus just wanted to do his job. He had been appointed by the Romans to replace Felix as governor of Judea, and in the transfer of leadership, he had inherited a unique prisoner named Paul.

Paul did not fit the reputation most people ascribe to prisoners. He was well educated and respectful, and he desired to live rightly before God and others. Why was he here?

The Jewish leaders had been hounding Festus to transfer Paul to Jerusalem to stand trial there—because they secretly wanted to assassinate him along the way. But Paul refused and appealed his case to Caesar. As Paul waited to leave for Rome, Festus discussed Paul's case with some visiting dignitaries and called for Paul to speak to them to help him make sense of the case. As Paul spoke, Festus became so puzzled by what Paul was saying about Jesus that he called Paul insane. Paul continued, however, and even tried to persuade the dignitaries themselves to become Christians.

After Paul was finished, the dignitaries informed Festus that Paul could have been set free if he had not appealed to Caesar, but Festus was now bound by Paul's appeal, so he sent him to Rome.

INFORMATION: The dignitaries who were visiting Festus were Agrippa II and his wife, Bernice. Agrippa II was the last of the descendants of Herod to rule over Judea, because it was during his reign that the First Jewish-Roman War occurred, and after that the Romans took more direct control over the region.

# GAAL
## Enemy of Gideon's Son Abimelek

Then Gaal son of Ebed said, "Who is Abimelek, and why should we
Shechemites be subject to him? Isn't he Jerub-Baal's son, and isn't
Zebul his deputy? Serve the family of Hamor, Shechem's father!
Why should we serve Abimelek?"

JUDGES 9:28

Many foolish ideas have been conceived in a bout of drinking and revelry, and
the result is usually the same: disaster. Such was the case with a man named Gaal
in the time of Israel's judges.

All we know about Gaal is that he was the son of a man named Ebed and
that he and his brothers moved into the area of Shechem sometime around the
time that Abimelek had become the leader of the region. Gaal must have been
a man of some influence as well, because he was able to stir up the leaders of
Shechem against Abimelek during a harvest festival when they were eating and
drinking in the temple of their god.

While Gaal was busy boasting of what he would do to Abimelek, however,
the governor of the city informed Abimelek of Gaal's ambitions. Abimelek then
advanced on the city in the morning, drew out Gaal and his men, and killed them
in battle. The next day he ruthlessly attacked the people of Shechem for support-
ing Gaal, and the very short story of Gaal and his ill-conceived idea came to an
end.

---

INFORMATION: The ancient city of Shechem played an
important role throughout the history of Israel. It was at Shechem that
the Lord revealed to Abraham that he would receive Canaan as his
inheritance (Genesis 12). Later Jacob bought a plot of ground there,
and Joseph's bones would eventually be laid to rest there (Genesis
33:18–19; Joshua 24:32). At Shechem the people established a
covenant with the Lord during the time of Joshua (Joshua 24). It was
also at Shechem that the kingdom of Israel split into two kingdoms
(1 Kings 12). And at a place near Shechem, Jesus spoke to a Samaritan
woman at Jacob's well (John 4).

# GAMALIEL
Jewish Rabbi and Paul's Mentor

But a Pharisee in the council named Gamaliel, a teacher of the law
held in honor by all the people, stood up and gave orders
to put the men outside for a little while.
ACTS 5:34 ESV

Gamaliel is a great example of the immense impact that a teacher—even an unbeliever—can have on the world. Gamaliel does not appear to have been a Christian, but through his student Saul/Paul he may well have had the greatest positive influence on Christianity of any unbeliever in history.

The Bible first mentions Gamaliel in connection with Peter and the other apostles, who were arrested for preaching in the name of Jesus Christ. Gamaliel, a respected teacher of Jewish law, persuaded the Sanhedrin to release the apostles and leave them alone—because if they were not from God, their cause would die out, just as many others had. But if they were from God, the Jewish leaders would be fighting against God Himself (Acts 5).

The only other time the Bible mentions Gamaliel is in a speech made by the apostle Paul. When Paul arrived in Jerusalem at the end of his third missionary journey, many Jews accused him of various offenses. Paul began his defense by recounting that he was educated by Gamaliel and was thoroughly trained in the law. He zealously persecuted Christians, but later the Lord appeared to him, and he became a Christian himself. Paul's thorough training in the law under Gamaliel's teaching eventually helped Paul to see how the law points to Jesus Christ, who fulfilled the law for us. Paul's ministry has helped to spread the good news of Jesus Christ throughout the world.

INTERESTING. . . Gamaliel was the grandson of Hillel, a famous teacher of religious law. Among other things, Hillel, who lived shortly before the time of Jesus, became well-known for stating a saying very similar to the Golden Rule (Matthew 7:12): "What is hateful to you, do not do to your fellow: this is the whole Law; the rest is the explanation; go and learn."

# GERSHOM
## First Son of Moses

The name of the one [son of Moses] was Gershom (for he said,
"I have been an alien in a foreign land").

EXODUS 18:3 NRSV

Gershom's story doesn't follow the expected plotline. It would be logical to assume that as the firstborn son of Moses, Gershom would rise to a significant position of leadership or power in the developing Hebrew nation. However, God did not choose Moses' children as his successors. Instead, in a surprising plot twist, God chose Joshua to lead His people into the Promised Land.

While still living in Midian, Moses and Zipporah welcomed Gershom into their family. Moses chose the name Gershom, which means "stranger" or "cast out," as a reference to his recent escape from Egypt. When God commissioned him to return to Egypt and lead the Israelites out of slavery, Moses took his wife and their son, Gershom, and began the journey to Egypt. On the way, Gershom became the object of an important lesson in obedience.

As a Hebrew, Moses should have circumcised his son, yet he had neglected to obey this command of God (Genesis 17). Before Moses could act as God's messenger, he needed to learn the importance of following God's commands himself. Fortunately, Zipporah recognized the error, moved quickly to circumcise their son, and averted God's judgment on their family.

INSIGHT: God doesn't value bloodlines like we often do. Instead, God looks at the heart of a person and builds His kingdom and plan around willing servants. That's an important reminder for children of Christian parents or for Christian parents as they raise their own children: Faith is not transferred like DNA. Each person must interact with God on his or her own initiative. Every individual is responsible for personally pursuing spiritual growth. No one inherits a relationship with God.

GIDEON twice asked God to confirm His call, by "putting out a fleece." One time, Gideon asked God to drop dew on the wool but not on the ground around it. The other time, Gideon asked for dewy ground but dry wool.

# GIDEON
## Judge of Israel

And he said to him, "Please, Lord, how can I save Israel? Behold,
my clan is the weakest in Manasseh, and I am the least in my father's house."
And the LORD said to him, "But I will be with you, and you shall strike
the Midianites as one man."

JUDGES 6:15-16 ESV

In a world weaned on the idea that success comes to those who believe in themselves, Gideon is a welcome misfit. Believing in himself—or even in the power of God for that matter—seemed virtually foreign to Gideon before God used him to do great things.

During a time when the Midianites were oppressing God's people, the Lord appeared to Gideon and told him to rescue His people—but Gideon responded pessimistically with, "How can I save Israel? Behold, my clan is the weakest in Manasseh, and I am the least in my father's house" (Judges 6:15 ESV). When the Lord told him to tear down his father's pagan altar, Gideon did so—but at night out of fear of his family and the townspeople. As Gideon prepared to fight the Midianites, he asked God two different times to send a sign to confirm that this was His will (Judges 6:34–40).

Even with Gideon's rather meek display of faith, however, God used him to rout the Midianites. And apparently in the process, God wanted to teach Gideon a lesson in faith—because He whittled Gideon's army down from thirty-two thousand to three hundred before the battle took place. In the end, Israel was rescued from the Midianites, and Gideon became a judge over the people for the rest of his life.

INSIGHT: Gideon is living proof that it is not the greatness of our faith that makes the difference but the greatness of the One in whom we have faith. Likewise, Jesus once said, "If you have faith as small as a mustard seed, you can say to this mountain, 'Move from here to there,' and it will move. Nothing will be impossible for you" (Matthew 17:20). Take courage in the great God in whom we believe.

GOLIATH, knocked down by a stone from David's slingshot, will be finished off by his own sword. The painting is part of Michelangelo's Sistine Chapel masterpiece.

# GOLIATH
## Philistine Warrior Killed by David

And there came out from the camp of the Philistines a champion named
Goliath of Gath, whose height was six cubits and a span.

1 SAMUEL 17:4 ESV

It's often who you know that makes all the difference. From business to politics
to box seats at sold-out sporting events, making a simple connection to an important name is sometimes all you need to go from zero to a dream come true.
But the key, of course, is *who*—whose name are you able to drop?

Goliath, a giant from the Philistine city of Gath, mistakenly assumed that
the only names he needed were those of his people and his pagan gods (1 Samuel
17:8, 43). When the Philistines were preparing for battle against the Israelites,
Goliath presented himself as the Philistines' champion and challenged the Israelites to send their own champion to fight him in order to determine which
group would be victorious. He identified himself as a Philistine, and he wrongly
assumed that all the Israelite warriors were merely servants of Saul (1 Samuel
17:8). But the shepherd boy David knew better. He came to Goliath in the name
of the Lord, and this name would make all the difference (1 Samuel 17:43–47).

The Lord gave David victory over Goliath and the other Israelites victory
over the Philistine army, and Goliath's name—and the name of his gods—would
forever be associated with defeat.

INSIGHT: God has promised that those who hope in Him will not
be disappointed (Isaiah 49:23), for His name is above every name, and
He is the only One with the power to rescue all who call on Him (Acts
4:12). Have you called on this name for your salvation?

# GOMER
## Unfaithful Wife of the Prophet Hosea

So he married Gomer daughter of Diblaim,
and she conceived and bore him a son.
HOSEA 1:3

Gomer is one of those people we would rather not acknowledge that we know. Perhaps that's because she reminds us of ourselves in ways that we wish she didn't.

Gomer was the wife of the prophet Hosea, whom the Lord commanded to marry a "promiscuous woman" (Hosea 1:2). It is not clear whether she was unfaithful when Hosea married her or only became unfaithful after the wedding. Whatever the case, Gomer sadly demonstrated that Hosea chose correctly when he married her, for though she bore Hosea three children, she eventually left him for another lover. Later Hosea found her again and even bought her back so that she could be faithful to him once again (Hosea 3).

In all this, Gomer was a living allegory of the unfaithfulness of God's people. Israel had been chosen by God to be a covenant partner with Him, but they had been unfaithful to Him by worshipping other gods and embracing wickedness. The Lord desired for them to come back to Him, but they often refused.

INSIGHT: In what ways have you been like Gomer? How have you strayed from your commitment to be faithful to God and His covenant with you? Is He calling you to return to Him and be faithful to Him once again? Don't run from the joys that God offers His people as His bride—His faithful, covenant people.

# HABAKKUK
## Prophet of Judah

The prophecy that Habakkuk the prophet received. How long, LORD, must I call for help, but you do not listen? Or cry out to you, "Violence!" but you do not save?

HABAKKUK 1:1-2

With all the injustice and evil going on seemingly unchecked around us, many of us think to ourselves, *God, don't You see what's going on? Why don't You do something?* Most of us, though, are too afraid to actually speak these thoughts to God. But not Habakkuk. He boldly brought these questions to God, and God answered, though not necessarily as Habakkuk was expecting.

We know almost nothing about Habakkuk except that, based on his prophecy, he must have lived just before the Babylonians attacked Judah and sent the people into exile. But what we do know is that he was very troubled by the wickedness going on around him, and it made him wonder whether God really cared and why He did not seem to be doing anything about it.

God answered Habakkuk's questions by assuring him that He was already raising up the Babylonians to punish the wickedness going on around him in Judah. The problem was that the Babylonians seemed even more evil than the people of Judah, according to Habakkuk—so he brought this concern to God, too.

God answered Habakkuk's second question by assuring him that one day He would punish those who have oppressed others. Habakkuk responded with a song of praise for God's mercy and salvation.

INSIGHT: When we experience pain and suffering, we may wonder why God doesn't seem to be doing anything to help us. Like Habakkuk, we should bring those questions directly to God and trust Him to answer. Otherwise we will likely breed resentment and more doubt. God does care for His people (Matthew 6:25–34, 10:29–31), and we can trust that He is always working for our good (Romans 8:28–29).

# HANANIAH, MISHAEL, AND AZARIAH
## Also Known as Shadrach, Meshach, and Abednego

The king talked with them, and he found none equal to Daniel, Hananiah, Mishael and Azariah; so they entered the king's service.
DANIEL 1:19

When the Babylonian king scrutinized Hananiah, Mishael, and Azariah, he found them "ten times better" than all of his sorcerers and astrologers (Daniel 1:20). Their secret was simple: The king could transplant them to pagan Babylon—he could even give them pagan names—but Babylon would not remove God from their hearts.

As members of the Jewish aristocracy, these men were taken to Babylon about two decades before Jerusalem and its temple were destroyed. In Babylon, they were trained to serve the court of King Nebuchadnezzar. Their Hebrew names, which honored God, were replaced with names that honored Babylonian idols and their new king. The change was intended to remind them that they now belonged to Nebuchadnezzar, and that his goal was their assimilation—a natural response since the king interpreted his triumph over Jerusalem as the triumph of his gods over the Hebrew God. These friends were now expected to pay homage to the victorious idols of Babylon.

The religious devotion of these men came under fire at least twice. The first test came when they were ordered to eat from the royal table even though Nebuchadnezzar's food and drink had been offered to idols first. Clearly, eating this food would have signified submission to the Babylonian gods. The three friends refused—and were later vindicated when their spartan diet of vegetables and water proved superior to the choicest meals from the king's table.

Later these men—along with the rest of Babylon—were ordered to bow down to a golden image erected by Nebuchadnezzar. Once more they refused to trade their God for Babylonian idols, and once more they were vindicated. After Nebuchadnezzar had the trio thrown into a fiery furnace, they emerged without so much as the smell of soot on them.

INSIGHT: Daniel 2 reveals how these three men were successful at resisting Babylon's influence. While all the king's astrologers relied on superstition and idolatry, these men relied on prayer (see Daniel 2:17–18). Rather than look to the stars to reveal truth, they looked to the One who made the stars.

In another image by Gustave Dore, HANANIAH, MISHAEL, and AZARIAH are unharmed by the flames of King Nebuchadnezzar's "fiery furnace."

# HANNAH
## Mother of Samuel

In her deep anguish Hannah prayed to the LORD weeping bitterly. And she made a vow, saying, "LORD Almighty, if you will. . .not forget your servant but give her a son, then I will give him to the LORD for all the days of his life."
1 SAMUEL 1:10–11

One of the most moving passages of scripture is the story of Hannah, the mother of the prophet Samuel. In the span of two simple chapters, we find such heartfelt themes as the pain and longing of childlessness, the joy of childbirth, and the surrender of a child to God's service.

When we first read about Hannah, she has been unable to bear a child and is being taunted for this by her rival, Peninnah, who is the other wife of Hannah's husband. Hannah's sorrow and longing lead her to pray earnestly to God for a son, whom she promises to dedicate fully to God's service (1 Samuel 1).

God answers Hannah's prayer, and she gives birth to Samuel. True to her word, Hannah brings Samuel to the tabernacle after he is weaned and gives him over to God's service there. Instead of expressing sorrow at her loss of Samuel, however, Hannah praises God for answering her prayer for a son (1 Samuel 2:1–10). Hannah eventually bears more children, and Samuel becomes a great prophet and judge over Israel.

INTERESTING. . . When Hannah promised to give her son over to God's service (1 Samuel 1:11), she was probably offering to make him a Nazirite for his entire life. People dedicated as Nazirites were not allowed to cut their hair or drink alcohol (Numbers 6).

HANNAH received a great blessing from the Lord—
and she repaid it by giving her son, Samuel, back to Him.

# HEROD AGRIPPA
## King of Judea and Grandson of Herod the Great

It was about this time that King Herod arrested some who belonged to the church, intending to persecute them. He had James, the brother of John, put to death with the sword.
ACTS 12:1–2

The old saying is often true: "The apple doesn't fall far from the tree." Or in the case of Herod Agrippa I, the apple doesn't fall far from the grand-tree, Herod the Great.

Herod the Great, who was king over the land of Israel when Jesus was born, was notorious for his ruthlessness toward those who appeared to threaten his rule. Upon his death, the Romans divided his territory among some of his sons, who also took the title "Herod." Three other sons, including one named Aristobulus, were killed as the family members fought among themselves for the crown.

After Gaius Caligula became emperor of Rome, he appointed Agrippa, the son of Aristobulus, as king over the land of Israel and eventually granted him virtually all the land that his grandfather Herod the Great had ruled.

Unfortunately Agrippa appears to have acquired his grandfather's ruthless political jealousy. As the church began to grow, Herod Agrippa must have regarded these followers of Jesus as a threat to his rule, and he began to persecute them. He even killed James, the brother of John. Once Agrippa saw that this gained him favor with the Jewish leaders, he arrested Peter, but an angel allowed Peter to escape from prison unharmed.

Herod was struck down by an angel of the Lord when he allowed people to praise him as a god (Acts 12).

INFORMATION: Gaius Caligula and Agrippa had been raised together in Rome, where they became friends. Agrippa continued to support the promotion of Gaius as emperor, which explains why Gaius granted Agrippa rule over so much land in Israel.

# HEROD THE GREAT
## King of Judea

Then Herod, when he saw that he had been tricked by the wise men,
became furious, and he sent and killed all the male children in Bethlehem
and in all that region who were two years old or under,
according to the time that he had ascertained from the wise men.

MATTHEW 2:16 ESV

Herod the Great was a man of many contradictions. He was king of Judea, yet he himself was an Idumean (that is, an Edomite). He gained favor with the Jewish leaders by completely renovating the temple of the Lord and making it rival any pagan temple of its day, yet he also built many pagan gymnasiums and other Hellenistic buildings throughout Judea and Samaria. He was often particular to maintain at least the appearance of conformity to Jewish customs, yet he freely broke the sixth commandment by mercilessly killing any who threatened his rule—including his own wife and sons. This contradiction led one ancient writer to comment that he would rather be Herod's *hus* ("pig," considered unfit to eat for Jews) than his *huios* ("son").

Herod's actions regarding Jesus' birth, then, should come as no surprise to us. When wise men came from the East seeking to worship the newborn King Jesus, they first asked Herod where the child was. Herod led them to believe that he wanted to worship the child, too, all the while planning to kill Him. When the wise men left without telling Herod exactly where the baby was, he became furious and ordered all the baby boys two years and younger to be killed. Jesus' family escaped to Egypt until Herod had died, then returned to Nazareth, where His parents had lived before He was born.

INFORMATION: Several people were named Herod in the Bible. Herod the Great had several sons, including Antipas (who ruled over Galilee and Perea), Archelaus (who ruled over Judea and Samaria), and Philip (who ruled over the northeast corner of Palestine). Much later, Herod's grandson Agrippa ruled over much of Judea and Samaria, and still later Agrippa II ruled over portions of Palestine and Lebanon.

# HERODIAS
## Wife of Herod Antipas

For Herod himself had given orders to have John arrested, and he
had him bound and put in prison. He did this because of Herodias,
his brother Philip's wife, whom he had married.
MARK 6:17

Nothing stings quite like the truth. Perhaps that's why Herodias hated John the
Baptist so much.

At the age of twenty-three, Herodias divorced her husband, Philip, who was
also her uncle, and married Antipas, another uncle. Both men were sons of Herod
the Great, the king who ruled over Judea and Galilee when Jesus was born. John
the Baptist openly condemned Antipas for his marriage to Herodias, which caused
Herodias to nurse a deep hatred of John (Mark 6:17–20). She wanted to have John
killed, but Antipas regarded John as a holy man and feared what would happen if
he killed him.

But Herodias's hatred was unrelenting, and eventually she found a way to
have John killed. Herod held a banquet for his birthday, and Herodias's daughter
danced for his guests. Herod was so pleased that he offered her anything she
wished for, up to half his kingdom. Herodias told her to ask for the head of John
the Baptist on a platter, and she did.

Herod Antipas was very distressed at her request, but he did not want to go
back on his offer in front of his guests, so he carried out her evil wishes immediately.

INFORMATION: A few years after Jesus' death, Herodias's
brother Agrippa was made king over certain parts of Palestine,
and she grew jealous. She urged Antipas to sail for Rome and ask
Emperor Caligula for the title of king. Agrippa, however, sent letters
denouncing Antipas for various misdeeds, and the emperor exiled him
to the area now known as France. Herodias chose to accompany him,
and she likely died there.

# HEZEKIAH
## King of Judah

[Hezekiah] held fast to the LORD and did not stop following him;
he kept the commands the LORD had given Moses. And the LORD was with him;
he was successful in whatever he undertook.

2 KINGS 18:6–7

Just as the darkest backdrops make diamonds sparkle the brightest, the dark days surrounding Hezekiah's reign made his godly life all the more brilliant.

Hezekiah's own father had promoted idolatry throughout Judah and had made Judah a subservient kingdom to the wicked Assyrian Empire (1 Kings 16). When Hezekiah assumed the throne of Judah at the age of twenty-five, the northern kingdom of Israel was only a few years away from being sent into exile for their wickedness (2 Kings 18:9–10). These were dark days indeed.

But Hezekiah determined to follow the Lord with all his heart, and the Lord empowered him to do great things for His people even in the midst of the evil forces that were still at work. Hezekiah removed idolatry from the land, including all the pagan items from the temple (2 Kings 18). He restored proper worship at the temple and sent invitations to everyone throughout the land—even people living in the northern kingdom of Israel—to come to Jerusalem to celebrate the Passover once again (2 Chronicles 29–30).

Not long after the northern kingdom of Israel fell to the Assyrians, the Assyrians attacked Jerusalem as well, but the Lord struck down 185,000 of their soldiers in a single night, and Jerusalem was spared (2 Kings 19:35–36).

INFORMATION: As part of his preparations for the Assyrian attack on Jerusalem, Hezekiah constructed a water tunnel to carry water from the Gihon Spring to the pool at the lower end of the city (2 Kings 20:20). The tunnel still exists today, and in 1838 an ancient inscription was found in it that commemorated its construction.

# HIRAM
## King of Tyre

Hiram king of Tyre had supplied Solomon with cedar and cypress timber
and gold, as much as he desired, King Solomon gave to
Hiram twenty cities in the land of Galilee.

1 KINGS 9:11 ESV

Great business executives are constantly on the lookout for win-win alliances
with other key businesses, and King Hiram of Tyre was a business leader par
excellence.

Hiram was king over the tiny island fortress of Tyre in modern-day Lebanon, but it would be a mistake to think that his small city was also small in power
and wealth. Under the leadership of Hiram and those who came after him, Tyre
grew into a world-renowned trading empire, like an ancient version of the New
York Stock Exchange. Tyre also capitalized on Lebanon's vast forests of highly
prized cedar and its abundance of skilled carpenters and stonemasons.

During David's and Solomon's days, Hiram forged alliances with Israel, no
doubt to ensure both peace with them and access to the key trade routes that
passed through Israel's territory. Hiram supplied cedar, trimmed stones, and
skilled labor for the building of the Lord's temple, and Solomon provided him
with food as well as twenty cities in Galilee (1 Kings 5). Later Hiram would
partner with Solomon in several trading expeditions to faraway places, bringing
back gold, silver, and exotic goods (1 Kings 9:26–28; 10:22). These alliances and
expeditions resulted in great wealth for both Hiram and Solomon.

INTERESTING. . .Tyre was originally two distinct cities, one
located on the mainland and the other on a small island just off the
coast. In 332 BC, however, Alexander the Great conquered the city by
building a causeway from the mainland almost to the island fortress.
Over time the causeway continued to silt up and permanently turned
the island into a peninsula, as it is today.

# HULDAH
## Prophetess During King Josiah's Reign

So Hilkiah the priest, and Ahikam, and Achbor, and Shaphan, and Asaiah
went to Huldah the prophetess, the wife of Shallum the son of Tikvah,
son of Harhas, keeper of the wardrobe (now she lived in Jerusalem
in the Second Quarter), and they talked with her.

2 KINGS 22:14 ESV

Everyone wants a straight shooter when in a tight spot, because the only words
that have a chance of bringing real help are those that give an honest assessment
of the situation. The prophetess Huldah was just the person Josiah needed when
all Israel was in a tight spot.

In the years leading up to Josiah's time, the people of Israel had been sin-
ning rampantly and repeatedly, and their actions were leading God to bring the
judgments warned about in Deuteronomy 27–28. Things had gotten so bad that
apparently even a book of the Law (what we would call the Bible) had been
completely lost (2 Kings 22:8–13).

When this book was found during extensive temple renovations, it was read
to King Josiah, and it told of the terrible judgments that awaited God's people
because of their disobedience. Josiah knew right away that this was serious, and
he needed someone who could tell him the truth about just what the nation was
facing—he needed to hear the words of the prophetess Huldah.

Huldah told Josiah's officials that the nation would indeed experience judgment, but Josiah himself would be spared this judgment, as it would occur after
his death. After this, Josiah went throughout the country, tearing down pagan
shrines and abolishing idolatry wherever he found it. Eventually the Lord still
brought judgment on the nation because of the sin of the people and their leaders, but Josiah was able to delay this punishment and promote godliness in his
lifetime.

INFORMATION: The Bible says that Huldah lived in the second
district of Jerusalem. This was a relatively new section of the city that
had developed as the city expanded westward. Hezekiah had enclosed
this portion of the city with a new wall many decades earlier.

# HUR
## The Hero from Behind the Scenes

But Moses' hands grew weary, so they took a stone and put it under him, and he sat on it, while Aaron and Hur held up his hands, one on one side, and the other on the other side. So his hands were steady until the going down of the sun.

EXODUS 17:12 ESV

Acts of heroism may come disguised as fairly simple gestures.

While Joshua and his army wielded their swords and shields against the Amalekites, the true heroes that day observed the fight from the top of a nearby hill. The Bible records that Moses, Aaron, and Hur climbed a hill in the vicinity of the conflict in order to watch Israel fight at Rephidim. With the battle raging below, Moses raised his hands in prayer to God. As long as Moses kept his hands raised, Israel secured the upper hand in the battle. But when Moses grew tired and lowered his hands, the Amalekites began to win the battle.

Hur became a military hero that day by faithfully doing the simplest of tasks: helping Moses raise his tired arms. After finding a rock for Moses to sit on, Aaron stood on one side of Moses and Hur on the other. Together they held his arms up until the sun set. Because of Hur's unpretentious contribution, the Israelites crushed the enemy army.

In addition to his place in this story, Hur is also noted as serving as a leader to the people. When Moses went to Mount Sinai, he left Aaron and Hur behind as his representatives to handle disputes and conflicts that might arise while he was gone (Exodus 24:14).

INFORMATION: Descendants of Esau, the Amalekites lived near the desert region of Paran—which lies along the southern border of the Promised Land. In addition to the battle involving Hur, the Amalekites skirmished with Israel during the time of the judges (Judges 8). They remained Israel's enemies until King David finally soundly defeated them(1 Samuel 15, 27, 30; 2 Samuel 8).

HUR was undoubtedly experienced with a sword, but he was also wise enough to know that no weapon he could wield would be as powerful as God's support.

# HYMENAEUS
## Early Christian Who Spread False Teaching

Their teaching will spread like gangrene. Among them are Hymenaeus and Philetus, who have departed from the truth. They say that the resurrection has already taken place, and they destroy the faith of some.
2 TIMOTHY 2:17–18

Does theology really matter? Doesn't it actually divide the church, rather than unite it and build it up? This common criticism toward doctrine, or official beliefs and teachings of the church, may sound appealing at first—but a careful look at a man named Hymenaeus should help us see that theology is indeed important and even critical to a healthy church.

What the Bible tells us about Hymenaeus is not good. Apparently he and two other men named Alexander and Philetus were stirring up the church in Ephesus with their teaching about the resurrection. It seems that Hymenaeus was teaching that the resurrection—the day when all the dead are raised to life and eternal judgment—had already taken place. It is not certain whether this means that he was saying that the day had come and gone and that they had missed the event, or that somehow the resurrection occurred as part of their acceptance of new life in Christ. In any case, it was upsetting some other believers, who were no doubt confused and concerned by all this.

So did Paul simply downplay the significance of the teaching about the resurrection? Did he say that Hymenaeus is entitled to his beliefs? No. Paul described the effect of his teaching as "gangrene" (2 Timothy 2:17). In another passage, Paul also spoke of Hymenaeus as having been "handed over to Satan to be taught not to blaspheme" (1 Timothy 1:20), which might have had to do with his teaching as well.

INFORMATION: It is not known for sure exactly what Paul meant by "handed over to Satan" when speaking of Hymenaeus's punishment. Most scholars take it to mean some form of excommunication or conditional expulsion from the church to lead him to repent of his actions.

# IBZAN
## Judge of Israel

After him, Ibzan of Bethlehem led Israel. He had thirty sons and thirty daughters. He gave his daughters away in marriage to those outside his clan, and for his sons he brought in thirty young women as wives from outside his clan.

JUDGES 12:8-9

Whatever the reason for his actions, Ibzan must have been a man of firm convictions. Ibzan was a judge of Israel for seven years after Jephthah of Gilead. Ibzan was from Bethlehem, but the Bible doesn't make it clear whether this was the same Bethlehem where David was born or another Bethlehem in the far north of Israel. In any case, Ibzan had thirty sons and thirty daughters, which suggests he was very wealthy and was a man of great influence.

The only other significant information we know about Ibzan is that he purposely arranged for each of his children to marry someone from "outside"—giving his daughters away to men from "outside," and bringing in women from "outside" to marry his sons (Judges 12:8–10). The Bible doesn't say specifically what "outside the clan" means, but it is likely that this meant someone who was still within their tribe. It is unlikely that he would have arranged for his children to marry non-Israelites.

By marrying his sons and daughters to people outside his clan, Ibzan may have been broadening his sphere of influence within his tribe, thereby elevating his status and perhaps even leading to his installment as a judge over Israel.

INFORMATION: Jewish tradition associates Ibzan with Boaz of Bethlehem (in Judah), who married Ruth and bore a son who became the grandfather of King David.

Most artistic depictions of Isaac show him as the boy almost sacrificed by his father, Abraham. In this image, an elderly, almost-blind ISAAC gives a blessing to his younger son, Jacob, posing as the older son, Esau.

# ISAAC
## Son of Abraham and Father of Jacob

Isaac reopened the wells that had been dug in the time of his father Abraham, which the Philistines had stopped up after Abraham died, and he gave them the same names his father had given them.

GENESIS 26:18

In a world that celebrates pioneers and trailblazers, it is easy to underestimate the importance of those who faithfully carry on what others have established. But a brief look at the life of Isaac, the son of Abraham and father of Jacob, will show that such people are just as critical to God's plan as those who are marking a new trail for others.

Isaac's greatest claim to fame was simply that he was the son of Abraham and Sarah, the child that was promised by the Lord to carry on Abraham's name and make him into a great nation.

As a young man, Isaac was nearly sacrificed by his father in a test of obedience, but at the last second the Lord stopped Abraham and showed him a ram to sacrifice instead. Later Abraham acquired a wife for Isaac from Haran, the land of his ancestors, and Isaac and Rebekah gave birth to the twins Esau and Jacob.

Much of Isaac's adult life consisted simply of maintaining and bolstering the abundance handed down to him by his father. He continued to look after his extensive herds of livestock, and he repeatedly reopened wells that his father had dug that had been stopped up by jealous neighbors.

In his later years, Isaac bestowed his blessing on his sons and unwittingly granted the greater blessing of birthright to the younger son, Jacob, who had deceived him into thinking he was the older son.

INSIGHT: It is often tempting to think that we are nothing if we are not making waves. But the simple faithfulness of Isaac makes it clear that some of us are simply called to be devoted followers and faithful managers of the things handed down by others. Make a point to appreciate the role such people play, whether that be your role or the role of others around you.

Bishop Gregory of Nyssa believed that ISAIAH "knew more perfectly than all others the mystery. . . of the gospel." Pretty impressive, considering Isaiah lived some seven hundred years before Jesus was born.

# ISAIAH
## Prophet of Israel and Judah

Then I [Isaiah] said, "For how long, Lord?" And he answered:
"Until the cities lie ruined and without inhabitant, until the houses are left
deserted and the fields ruined and ravaged, until the LORD has sent
everyone far away and the land is utterly forsaken."

ISAIAH 6:11–12

"Wanted: dedicated employee who will faithfully proclaim messages of judgment to people who will reject and despise you. All efforts will produce little noticeable results and will end in complete destruction." It's unlikely that a job posting like that would garner many applicants. Yet that is essentially the job to which the prophet Isaiah was called by God.

Isaiah was probably closely affiliated with the royal court, given his relatively easy access to the king (Isaiah 7:3). But at some point in his life, the Lord, in His royal splendor, appeared to him in a vision (Isaiah 6), and Isaiah's life was forever changed. He was called to prophesy God's messages of judgment and restoration to His people, but God also warned him that the people would not listen and would eventually experience destruction. Even Isaiah's own children bore prophetic names: Shear-Jashub ("A Remnant Shall Return") and Maher-Shalal-Hash-Baz ("Swift Is Spoil, Speedy Is Prey").

Isaiah faithfully carried out his solemn and weighty task to the very end. He began prophesying a few decades before the fall of the northern kingdom of Israel and ended a few decades after this event.

Isaiah's efforts were not really futile, though, for his words were recorded for later generations in the book of Isaiah. Many of these prophecies foretold the Messiah, who would redeem His people from their bondage.

INFORMATION: Isaiah is the Old Testament book most quoted in the New Testament. Jesus quoted Isaiah 6:9–10, which speaks of the people's callous hearts, when His disciples asked why He spoke in parables rather than in direct statements (Matthew 13:13–15).

# ISHMAEL
## Son of Abraham

"And as for Ishmael, I have heard you: I will surely bless him; I will make him fruitful and will greatly increase his numbers. He will be the father of twelve rulers, and I will make him into a great nation."
GENESIS 17:20

When we are seeking the will of God but run into a roadblock, we may start to ask, *Have I made a wrong turn? Will I miss out on God's good plan for me? Has God changed His mind? Should I come up with a plan B?* These questions were no doubt on Abraham's mind, too, as he contemplated God's plans for him and for his son, Ishmael.

God had promised to bless Abraham and make his descendants into a great nation, a chosen people of God (Genesis 12:1–3; 15:1–6). But Sarah, Abraham's wife, was about seventy-six years old and had not yet borne any children. So, in keeping with ancient Near Eastern customs, Sarah offered her handmaid, Hagar, to bear a child for Abraham—and Ishmael was born. Based on Abraham's limited knowledge at that point, he had no reason to think that Ishmael was not the fulfillment of God's promises. But later God made it clear that it would be through Sarah herself that God's chosen people would come (Genesis 17).

So what about Ishmael? Did he have any significance in his own right? Or would he simply be cast aside by God as a leftover plan B?

Not at all. Though he was not to be the ancestor of God's chosen people, Ishmael was in fact part of God's plan as well. He would become the father of another great nation (Genesis 17:20), traditionally believed to be the Arab peoples.

INSIGHT: The will of God for our future can be a difficult thing to discern clearly, and we may even find that what we thought was God's will was not. As we continue to seek His will, however, we can rest assured that God is always working, and what may seem like "wrong" turns are in fact part of God's good plan as well (Romans 8:28).

Forced into the wilderness, ISHMAEL swoons as his mother, Hagar, worries. Caught in the middle of Abraham and Sarah's struggle to obey God, Ishmael will survive thanks to God's intervention—and become a great nation himself.

# JABEZ
## Man Who Asked for God's Blessing

Jabez cried out to the God of Israel, "Oh, that you would bless me and enlarge my territory! Let your hand be with me, and keep me from harm so that I will be free from pain." And God granted his request.

1 CHRONICLES 4:10

Imagine having a name like Pain or Trouble, a permanent reminder of the sorrow that you brought your mother at birth. Wouldn't it make you want to redeem yourself somehow in the eyes of your parents and others? This reality may be part of the background in Jabez's story.

The Bible says that Jabez was a descendant of Judah and that he was more honorable than his brothers. It doesn't even say why he was more honorable, but we can probably assume that it is because of the noble prayer he offered to God.

Jabez's name sounds like the Hebrew word for *pain*, which explains why his mother gave him that name when she bore him in pain. The social stigma that Jabez endured because of his name's associations must have been great, because he prayed that God would do various things that would redeem his name. He prayed that God would bless him and enlarge his territory, meaning that God would grant him even more land than that which had been granted to his family as part of their original inheritance in the Promised Land. He also asked that God's hand, presumably of blessing and protection, would be with him and that He would keep him from harm. In this way he would be free from pain.

INSIGHT: You may not have an actual name like Pain or Trouble, but perhaps your name—that is, your reputation—has become permanently associated with some other negative characteristic, and you desire to redeem your reputation. Ask God to bless you and help you to overcome whatever negative traits have been associated with your name.

# JABIN

## Canaanite King Who Oppressed God's People

And the hand of the Israelites grew stronger and stronger against Jabin,
the Canaanite king, until they destroyed him.

JUDGES 4:24

David once sang, "Some trust in chariots and some in horses, but we trust in the name of the Lord our God" (Psalm 20:7). David's timeless words would have been just as fitting for Jabin—two hundred years earlier—as they were for himself.

King Jabin of Hazor had plenty of horses and chariots—nine hundred to be exact (Judges 4:3)—but they were not enough to stop God's hand leading His people to victory against him. When Jabin began to oppress God's people, the Lord instructed his prophet Deborah to call for a man named Barak to lead God's people into battle. Barak led his men to Mount Tabor, while Jabin's commander, Sisera, led his forces toward him in the valley of Jezreel along the Kishon River. Barak's men rushed down the mountain and routed Sisera's forces, chasing them all the way back to their homes. Even Sisera had to flee on foot and was eventually killed by a woman as he slept (Judges 4–5).

That battle appears to have marked the beginning of the end for Jabin's rule over the Israelites (Judges 4:24).

INFORMATION: Mount Tabor and the valley of Jezreel were the site of another important battle during the time of the judges. Gideon and his small army of three hundred men were victorious in a battle against the vast Midianite army in this area (Judges 8:18). Hundreds of years later, Alexander the Great captured a fortress called Itabyrium located on the top of Mount Tabor.

JACOB dreams of a ladder to heaven, a vision in which God reiterated His vow to give the "promised land" to Jacob and his descendants.

# JACOB

## Son of Isaac and Father of the Israelite Tribes

After this, his brother came out, with his hand grasping Esau's heel; so he was named Jacob. Isaac was sixty years old when Rebekah gave birth to them.
GENESIS 25:26

It's not uncommon for parents to give their children names that express the hopes they have for them or the attributes they associate with them: Joy, Hope, Victor, Hunter, and so on. So how about the idea of *Deceiver*? That's exactly the sentiment expressed by the name Jacob.

Jacob, also called Israel, was the son of Isaac and the father of the twelve patriarchs of Israel. He and his older brother, Esau, were twins—and when they were born, Jacob was grasping the heel of Esau (Genesis 25:26), so he was given the name Jacob ("heel holder"). In ancient Israel, to "grasp the heel" meant to deceive or supplant, which was somewhat fitting for Jacob's personality throughout much of his life.

Some of the ways that Jacob deceived or supplanted others include convincing Esau to trade his birthright for a bowl of stew (Genesis 25:29–34), tricking Isaac to gain the blessing he wanted to give Esau (Genesis 27), and fooling his uncle Laban to increase his flocks (Genesis 30). Later, after Jacob wrestled with a man of God at the Jabbok River, his name was appropriately changed to Israel, meaning "one who strives with God" (Genesis 32).

One of Jacob's twelve sons was Joseph, who rose to a position of second in command of Egypt, and Jacob and his family moved to Egypt to live with him there. After Jacob had grown very old, he blessed his twelve sons and died (Genesis 37–50).

---

INFORMATION: Once, even Jacob the Deceiver was deceived by his uncle Laban. Jacob had worked for seven years to pay the bride price for Rachel, but Laban gave Jacob Rachel's older sister, Leah, instead. Jacob had to work another seven years for Rachel (Genesis 29).

---

Synagogue leaders may have seen Jesus as something of a rebel or troublemaker—but faced with the loss of a beloved child, JAIRUS instinctively looked to the Lord for help.

# JAIRUS
## Synagogue Official Whose Daughter Died

Then a man named Jairus, a synagogue leader, came and fell at Jesus' feet,
pleading with him to come to his house because his only daughter,
a girl of about twelve, was dying.

LUKE 8:41-42

It's the reason ambulances are allowed to run red lights and emergency rooms stand ready to deal with virtually any life-threatening situation: Life is fragile, and time is critical when emergencies arise. Surely this was what Jairus must have been thinking when he came to Jesus, fell at His feet, and pleaded for Him to come and heal his dying daughter (Luke 8:40–56). And if we find ourselves perplexed by Jesus as He took time to find out who touched His garment amid a great crowd, we are probably thinking the same thing about life.

But Jesus didn't see things that way. There is no mention of urgency in His pace, no mention of concern about whether they would reach the girl in time to help her. And even when someone informed Jesus along the way that Jairus's daughter had already died, no mention is made that Jesus expressed any despair. The Bible doesn't record Jairus's reaction, but he may have wondered whether Jesus really cared what happened to his daughter. But Jesus responded this way not because He was uncaring, but because He knew He had no reason to worry— His Father was in complete control of the situation (Luke 8:50).

When Jesus finally arrived at the house, He simply made His way to where the girl was, took her by the hand, and raised her to life again. Such is the power of God—and the reason that we, too, can always find great assurance and peace in Him.

INFORMATION: Jairus was said to be a "ruler of the synagogue," which probably meant that he was in charge of arranging the services for the local synagogue each Sabbath day. The book of Acts makes reference to two other people who were rulers of the synagogue (Acts 13:15; 18:8).

A half-brother of Jesus, JAMES—known as "James the Just" in some church traditions—is pictured in an icon from a Russian Orthodox church.

# JAMES
## Brother of Jesus and
## Leader of Jerusalem Church

Then after three years, I [Paul] went up to Jerusalem to get acquainted
with Cephas and stayed with him fifteen days. I saw none of the
other apostles—only James, the Lord's brother.
GALATIANS 1:18-19

James, often called James the Just, seems to be an enigma in virtually every way.
He is at the center of several controversies surrounding the history of the early
church.

What is generally agreed upon about James is that he was the leader of the
Jerusalem church, and he was in contact with such leaders as Peter, John, Barnabas, and Paul. At the first church council in Jerusalem, James was instrumental
in forging the church's position regarding Gentiles and the Law of Moses (Acts
15). Beyond this, it seems like everything else is in dispute.

Regarding his relationship to Jesus, there is debate whether he was Jesus'
half brother, Jesus' stepbrother, Jesus' cousin, or something else.

Regarding his theology, James's emphasis on works rather than faith alone
has led some to argue that he stands in opposition to Paul's emphasis on salvation
by grace through faith—but others argue that the two positions complement and
balance each other.

Regarding archaeological evidence of his existence, a controversy erupted in
2002 when a tomb purported to be his was made public, but later it was deemed
to be a fake by the Israeli Antiquities Authority.

Despite all these controversies, however, James's letter to the scattered believers has always been a favorite due to its very practical wisdom and instruction.
It is often referred to as the Proverbs of the New Testament.

INFORMATION: According to the Jewish historian Josephus,
the Sanhedrin charged James with breaking the law and stoned him to
death around AD 62.

# JANNES AND JAMBRES
## Pharaoh's Magicians Who Opposed Moses

But the magicians of Egypt did the same by their secret arts; so Pharaoh's heart remained hardened, and he would not listen to them; as the LORD had said.
EXODUS 7:22 NRSV

When Moses and Aaron confronted Pharaoh in Egypt, members of Pharaoh's court opposed them and tried to duplicate Moses and Aaron's miraculous signs. While the book of Exodus doesn't reveal the names of these rivals, Hebrew tradition preserves their memory as Jannes and Jambres—which the apostle Paul also affirms (2 Timothy 3:8).

God had given Moses and Aaron specific miracles to help persuade Pharaoh to release God's people from their slavery. By trying to duplicate these miracles, Pharaoh's magicians hoped to keep the people of God enslaved in Egypt.

Although Jannes and Jambres managed to copy many of God's miraculous signs, they could not do so universally. Exodus 8 records that these magicians failed to replicate the plague of gnats, and Exodus 9:11 records that the plague of boils had affected them so badly that they could not stand before Pharaoh.

Throughout Israel's history, these men served as an archetype of those who fight against the progress of God's plan and His gospel message. Paul wrote: "As Jannes and Jambres opposed Moses, so these people, of corrupt mind and counterfeit faith, also oppose the truth" (2 Timothy 3:8 NRSV). Their actions made these men appropriate symbols of opposition to God's deliverance of His people.

INTERESTING. . . These magicians became popular villains throughout Israel's history. Not only were their names preserved as the magicians of Pharaoh's court, but Hebrew tradition also refers to these men as sons of Balaam, as those who incited Aaron to build the golden calf, and as having died at the crossing of the Red Sea. Though physically impossible for Jannes and Jambres to be linked in actuality to each of these episodes, their mention in each reveals the place these men occupied in the Hebrews' hearts and minds.

# JEHOAHAZ
## King of Judah

Josiah's servants brought his body in a chariot from Megiddo to Jerusalem and buried him in his own tomb. And the people of the land took Jehoahaz son of Josiah and anointed him and made him king in place of his father.

2 KINGS 23:30

It's difficult to find any other word than *tragic* to describe the life of King Jehoahaz of Judah. The only bright spot in his life seems to be that he was born to Josiah, the great king of Judah who brought religious reform to Judah during the dark days immediately before the Babylonian exile. But even his father's connection was still marked by sorrow, for it was Josiah's tragic death in battle that led to Jehoahaz's ascension to the throne.

After Josiah died trying to stop Pharaoh Neco of Egypt from advancing to help the Assyrians, the people of the land—probably meaning the clan leaders—took Jehoahaz and made him king. Jehoahaz only reigned for three months, though, because Pharaoh Neco dethroned the new king and took him away to Egypt, where he eventually died. Then the Egyptians installed one of Jehoahaz's brothers as king instead and imposed a heavy tax on the people (2 Kings 23).

INFORMATION: Jehoahaz was one of the last of the descendants of David to rule over Judah. Only three other kings ruled after him, and after that the Babylonians invaded the land, exiling most of the nobles to Babylon (2 Kings 23–24).

# JEHOIAKIM
## King of Judah

In his days, Nebuchadnezzar king of Babylon came up, and Jehoiakim became his servant three years. Then he turned and rebelled against him.

2 KINGS 24:1 ESV

Jehoiakim's reign marked the beginning of the end for the kingdom of Judah. Jehoiakim was originally named Eliakim by his father, Josiah, but Pharaoh Neco of Egypt changed his name after he took his brother King Jehoahaz captive to Egypt and installed Jehoiakim as the new king. Jehoiakim was required to pay Pharaoh Neco a large sum of money, so he imposed a real estate tax to raise the money. The Bible characterizes Jehoiakim's reign as evil (2 Kings 23:34–36).

Later the Babylonians gained control over Judah, and at first Jehoiakim chose to make Judah a vassal, or dependent state, of Babylon, rather than risk challenging their rule. Three years later, however, Jehoiakim rebelled, and King Nebuchadnezzar exiled him and many other leaders to Babylon (2 Chronicles 36:6). Nebuchadnezzar then installed Jehoiakim's son as king, later deposing and exiling him, too, and installing Jehoiakim's brother as king. After that, the Babylonians broke down the walls of Jerusalem, and the temple itself was destroyed, bringing the kingdom of Judah to an end. For many years to come, the country would simply be a province of foreign powers.

INTERESTING. . . Daniel, Shadrach, Meshach, and Abednego were among those who were exiled to Babylon along with Jehoiakim (Daniel I). Though this exile was devastating to Judah as a country, and no doubt traumatic for those who were exiled, it appears that a few Judeans such as Daniel and his friends gained positions of leadership within the Babylonian government. Daniel's leadership even continued under the Persians, who conquered the Babylonians (Daniel 6:28).

# JEHU
## King of Israel

Jehu got up and went into the house. Then the prophet poured the oil on Jehu's head and declared, "This is what the LORD, the God of Israel, says: 'I anoint you king over the LORD's people Israel. You are to destroy the house of Ahab your master, and I will avenge the blood of my servants the prophets and the blood of all the LORD's servants shed by Jezebel.'"

2 KINGS 9:6-7

From bombing abortion clinics to spreading lies about political candidates, there are many ways God's people have gone wrong in their attempts to do right. Perhaps we should all take a lesson from the life of Jehu, king of Israel.

The Bible makes it clear that the Lord had appointed Jehu, the commander of Israel's troops, to bring an end to the reign of evil King Joram of Israel and to wipe out Ahab's family for its wickedness. The Lord even instructed the prophet Elisha to anoint Jehu for this very task (2 Kings 9). The problem was that Jehu appears to have allowed his zeal to turn into an unbridled lust for violence, and he eventually showed more interest in destroying others than in carrying out the Lord's will.

Jehu began his rampage by returning to Jezreel from battle and killing King Joram of Israel, King Ahaziah of Judah, and Jezebel, the widow of Ahab. Immediately after this, he went to Samaria and arranged for the death of seventy sons of Ahab (2 Kings 10). Then he killed forty-two relatives of King Ahaziah. Finally, he arranged for many of the prophets and priests of Baal to be assembled in the temple of Baal, and he slaughtered them all and destroyed the temple.

The Lord's disapproval of Jehu's excessiveness was made clear by the prophet Hosea, who said that the Lord would punish the house of Jehu for his massacre at Jezreel (Hosea 1:3).

INSIGHT: Have you ever allowed zeal for righteousness to disintegrate into simple hatred toward others? Don't misuse the name of the Lord by allowing your sinful desires to replace the Lord's call for promoting righteousness.

The victorious warrior JEPHTHAH recoils in horror at the sight of his daughter. He had made a foolish promise to God that, in return for military success, he would sacrifice the first thing that came out of the door of his home.

# JEPHTHAH
## Judge of Israel Who Made a Foolish Vow

And Jephthah made a vow to the LORD: "If you give the Ammonites into
my hands, whatever comes out of the door of my house to meet me
when I return in triumph from the Ammonites will be the LORD's,
and I will sacrifice it as a burnt offering."

JUDGES 11:30-31

In the book of Ecclesiastes, the teacher wisely instructed his listeners, "Do not
be quick with your mouth, do not be hasty in your heart to utter anything before
God. God is in heaven and you are on earth, so let your words be few" (Ecclesiastes 5:2). Unfortunately for Jephthah and his daughter, the teacher didn't write
those words until long after this story in Judges.

Jephthah lived during the time of Israel's judges, an outcast among his own
family because he was the son of a prostitute. Still, he had the opportunity to
make a name for himself when the leaders of Israel needed help fighting the
Ammonites, who were oppressing them. Jephthah agreed, but with the condition that he rule the people if he was victorious over the Ammonites. As he
was preparing to battle the enemy—no doubt calculating the high stakes of
the outcome—Jephthah made a rash vow to the Lord: He promised to sacrifice
the first thing that came out of his house to greet him if he won.

Jephthah was indeed victorious over the Ammonites, but when he returned
home, he was shocked to find his daughter, rather than some chicken or goat,
running out to greet him first. So Jephthah offered his daughter as a sacrifice
(Judges 11).

INTERESTING. . . In another battle against some of his fellow
Israelites, Jephthah and his men capitalized on a pronunciation
difference between the Ephraimites and the Gileadites. Whenever a
person wanted to cross one of Jephthah's checkpoints, he would have
to pronounce the word "Shibboleth." An Ephraimite could be detected
immediately, because he would be unable to pronounce the *sh* sound
and would pronounce the word as "Sibboleth."

# JESUS
## Son of God

"For even the Son of Man did not come to be served, but to serve, and to give his life as a ransom for many."
MARK 10:45

The list of paradoxes about Jesus seems endless—born to die, fully God and fully man, served others though He was King of kings, betrayed to death by a kiss—but perhaps the greatest paradox is also the most wonderful for us: He died so that we might receive life.

Even Jesus' beginnings are difficult to describe, because as the third person of the Trinity, He has always existed (see John 1:1–3; 8:58). In terms of His earthly life, however, Jesus was born to Mary and Joseph, who descended from King David himself (Matthew 1–2; Luke 2–3). Jesus grew up in the town of Nazareth and became a carpenter, like Joseph (Matthew 13:55; Mark 6:3).

Jesus began His public ministry of teaching and healing around age thirty (Luke 3:23), and His ministry lasted about three years. At the end of His ministry, some jealous Jewish leaders, looking for a way to get rid of Him, accused Him of treason before the Roman governor for His claim to be the Messiah, the King of the Jews. The Romans crucified Jesus along with two bandits, and He was buried in a borrowed rock tomb (Matthew 26–27).

Three days later, God raised Jesus to life again, just as He had promised. Later Jesus ascended to heaven until the time comes for Him to return to take His followers with Him to heaven (Matthew 28; Luke 24:50–53).

INSIGHT: To read the bare facts about Jesus' life and death can mislead us into seeing Him as another tragic victim of an evil world—but the truth is that the world was merely carrying out the plan of God for the salvation of His people (Acts 2). Through Jesus' death, the price for sin was paid, and we can be made right with God (Romans 5). Praise God for sending Jesus to bring us eternal life in Him!

"Behold the man." Pilate offers JESUS to the people, and they demand His death. At right, a woman, perhaps Pilate's wife, who had dreamed of Jesus, turns away in despair.

# JEREMIAH
## Prophet of Judah

"Do not be afraid of them, for I am with you and will rescue you," declares the Lord. Then the Lord reached out his hand and touched my [Jeremiah's] mouth and said to me, "Now, I have put my words in your mouth."
JEREMIAH 1:8-9

No one wants to be the one to pass on bad news, especially if the people you are speaking to don't really want to hear the truth. But this was the painful ministry that the prophet Jeremiah was called to even before he was born (Jeremiah 1:5).

Jeremiah was probably only about twenty years old when the Lord informed him of his special calling to prophesy against His people. At first Jeremiah was reluctant, but the Lord told him not to fear the people, for He would be with him (Jeremiah 1:17–19). Jeremiah began his ministry in the days of the godly king Josiah, but he would eventually witness the destruction of Jerusalem and the temple at the hands of the Babylonians. All the while, he faithfully warned the people of the impending consequences of their wickedness and idolatry.

Jeremiah was often perceived as a traitor for preaching his messages of doom. Once some royal officials of Judah even put Jeremiah in an empty cistern until he was rescued by a Cushite named Ebed-Melech (Jeremiah 38).

After the Babylonians attacked Jerusalem and destroyed the temple, some fleeing Judeans took Jeremiah with them to Egypt, where he prophesied more messages of doom and probably spent the rest of his life.

INSIGHT: Have you ever faced a situation where you had to warn others about the consequences of their actions? Even if the people you are speaking to become angry or threaten you with harm, you do not need to fear—the Lord is with you, just as He was with Jeremiah.

# JETHRO
## Moses' Father-in-Law

So Moses listened to his father-in-law and did all that he had said.
EXODUS 18:24 NASB

Once Jethro gave his daughter to Moses in marriage, he didn't expect her to move back home. Moses had shown kindness to Jethro's family, and Jethro welcomed him into his home and rewarded him with marriage to Zipporah, one of his seven daughters. The marriage gave Jethro confidence that his daughter would be cared for after he died. He must have been surprised when she arrived at his home while Moses was still alive and well.

Earlier in their story, they all lived together in Midian. At one point, God called Moses to return and lead the Hebrew people out of captivity. Jethro blessed Moses, said good-bye to his daughter and grandchildren, and sent them all on their journey back to Egypt. Moses, his wife, and their children endured the journey, witnessed the plagues brought on the Egyptians, and walked through the Red Sea together.

Though we don't know Moses' reasons, we read that he sent his wife and children back to Midian to live with Jethro after God miraculously delivered the Hebrews from Egypt. Perhaps Moses felt the upcoming journey would be too difficult or too dangerous for his family. Or perhaps he felt his own responsibilities would keep him from caring for his family properly. While we don't know his reasons, we do know that Jethro did not accept his daughter and grandchildren back as permanent guests but rather escorted them back to their proper place with Moses (Exodus 18).

Moses greatly respected Jethro and received his family back from him. And while Jethro visited with Moses, he helped God's leader prioritize and delegate (Exodus 18:13–23).

INTERESTING. . . Jethro's wise counsel proved to be a valuable lesson early in Moses' forty-year ministry of leading God's people. Jethro was also known as Reuel, which was probably his given name. The name Jethro was actually a title, which means "His Excellence." Jethro is referred to by both names in Exodus and Numbers.

JOANNA is among the group of women who first heard of Jesus' resurrection from an angel at the empty tomb. This 1889 sculpture is by Antonio Brilla.

# JOANNA
## Woman Who Supported Jesus' Ministry

It was Mary Magdalene, Joanna, Mary the mother of James, and the others with them who told this to the apostles. But they did not believe the women, because their words seemed to them like nonsense.

LUKE 24:10-11

There are people in the Bible who are marked by some very intriguing contrasts. Take Joanna, for example. She was the wife of Chuza, Herod's household manager—which means that she must have been very wealthy and powerful compared to most other women in first-century Palestine. This also means that her husband was directly connected to the very man who put John the Baptist to death and who played a role in Jesus' death. Yet she was also among those who followed Jesus faithfully and financially provided for Him and His disciples. Her husband must have known and likely supported her association with Jesus. Perhaps this is one of the ways that Herod had become acquainted with Jesus' activities (Luke 23:8).

Because of her close relationship to Jesus and to the other women who followed Him, Joanna was among those who witnessed Jesus' crucifixion and were first told by angels of Jesus' resurrection. Yet her high societal status and her financial support of Jesus and His disciples did not stop the disciples from dismissing her report about the resurrection as nonsense. They insisted on going to the tomb themselves to see what was going on (Luke 24:10–11).

INTERESTING. . . It seems that Jesus must have cured Joanna of an evil spirit or a disease (Luke 8:2), which may be why she became such a devoted supporter of Jesus' ministry.

JOB, as envisioned by the Mexican painter Gonzalo Carrasco. God allowed Satan to attack Job's possessions, family, and own body—but Job refused to "curse God and die" as his wife suggested.

# JOB
## Man of Suffering

In the land of Uz there lived a man whose name was Job. This man was
blameless and upright; he feared God and shunned evil.

JOB 1:1

Suffering the consequences of our wrong actions can be painful, but it pales in
comparison to the pain that we feel when we suffer for no apparent reason of our
own. That is why Job's painful experiences move us so deeply.

Job was a very successful man, with seven sons, three daughters, and a wealth
of livestock. In fact, "he was the greatest man among all the people of the East"
(Job 1:3). The Bible also makes it clear that Job was a righteous man. In a single
day, however, nearly all his earthly blessings were snatched away: All his animals
were either stolen or destroyed, and every single one of his children died in a terrible tragedy. Yet "in all this, Job did not sin by charging God with wrongdoing"
(1:22).

But Job's sufferings were not over yet. He himself was stricken with terrible
sores from head to toe, and even his own wife prodded him to give up on God
(Job 2). Finally, some of Job's friends came to mourn with him; but in the end,
each of them spent great energy trying to convince Job that he had caused his
own suffering by some hidden sin.

In all of this, God was holding Job up as an example of a truly righteous
man, someone who would remain faithful even when undergoing terrible suffering. That does not mean that Job did not question what God was doing and
express anger over his condition. When God finally did answer Job, however,
He made it clear that His ways are far above human ways and cannot truly be
understood by human beings.

Job humbly recognized his place before God, and God blessed him once
again with even more children and livestock.

INFORMATION: The book of Job is written in both poetry
and prose. The prose sections include the introductory section (which
sets the scene and informs the reader of the dialogue between God
and Satan) and the conclusion (which describes Job's restoration and
blessing). The rest of the book is written in Hebrew poetry.

A mother's love for her children—like JOCHEBED's for Moses—is one of the most powerful forces in the world. It's a limited but beautiful reflection of God's love for His own children.

# JOCHEBED
## Mother of Moses, Aaron, and Miriam

The name of Amram's wife was Jochebed daughter of Levi, who was born to
Levi in Egypt; and she bore to Amram: Aaron, Moses, and their sister Miriam.
NUMBERS 26:59 NRSV

Jochebed was a risk-taker. Although the Bible doesn't give us a detailed biography of Moses' mother, it does disclose the results of the courageous choices she made.

When the Egyptian Pharaoh ordered the death of all newborn Hebrew boys in order to slow the slaves' population growth, Jochebed took decisive action to protect the life of her tiny son. The risks she took on Moses' behalf often go unnoticed:

- Jochebed risked punishment by defying the king's orders and letting her son live.
- She secretly hid her newborn baby for three months (Exodus 2:2).
- She risked her child's life by placing the infant in a floating basket in the Nile. She could not have known if this daring action would result in the baby being lost downstream, being discovered and killed, being drowned, being eaten by Nile crocodiles, or being discovered and spared.
- She risked exposure by having Miriam, her daughter, watch the basket and then approach the Egyptian princess with an offer of aid.

Though bold, Jochebed's choices were not reckless. A descendant of Levi, she had faith that God could intervene and save the boy she viewed as "a fine baby" (Exodus 2:2 NRSV).

INSIGHT: Faith can be risky. We don't know what other risks Jochebed may have taken and how those turned out, but we do know that in this case God fulfilled His plan for the Hebrew people because of the risks she took. Doing what is right isn't always easy, and it can often be accompanied by a fair amount of risk. But when faith-based risks and God's plan coincide, the results can change the world.

JOHN's position as the youngest disciple is usually indicated in art by his lack of a beard. According to church tradition, he was the only one of the group to reach old age and die of natural causes.

# JOHN
## Apostle

*When Jesus saw his mother there, and the disciple whom he loved standing nearby, he said to her, "Woman, here is your son."*
JOHN 19:26

"The disciple whom [Jesus] loved." What title could anyone possibly want more than this? This title was the distinct privilege of the apostle John, the writer of the Gospel and letters that bear his name (John 13:23; 19:26; 21:7, 20).

We first read about John when he is chosen along with his brother James to leave his profession as a fisherman and become one of Jesus' disciples. John and his brother must have been somewhat of a rowdy pair, because Jesus nicknamed them "Sons of Thunder" (Mark 3:17). Nevertheless, John held some special place in Jesus' heart, because he was included in Jesus' "inner circle" of followers (Mark 5:37; 9:2; 13:3; 14:33) and was specifically given the responsibility to take care of Jesus' mother as Jesus neared death (John 19:26–27).

Soon after Jesus' resurrection, John and Peter healed a crippled man and were thrown into prison for preaching in the name of Jesus (Acts 3–4). Later John and Peter were sent to Samaria to confirm the genuineness of some Samaritans' conversion to Christianity (Acts 8). Years later John apparently moved to Ephesus, where he established his ministry among the churches of western Asia Minor. Near the end of his life, John was exiled to the island of Patmos off the coast of Asia Minor, and there he wrote the book of Revelation, a vision of the final days of the world.

INSIGHT: While John's title as "the disciple whom Jesus loved" certainly sets him apart as one who enjoyed a special relationship with Jesus, all believers in a sense can also claim this privileged title, for we are all followers (disciples) whom Jesus loves.

JOHN baptizes Jesus as the rest of the Trinity—represented by the Father's hands and a dove as the Holy Spirit—watch over the ceremony. The painting is by Leonardo Da Vinci.

# JOHN THE BAPTIST
## Forerunner of Jesus

John replied in the words of Isaiah the prophet, "I am the voice of one calling in the wilderness, 'Make straight the way for the Lord.'"
JOHN 1:23

John the Baptist was a man who clearly understood his calling: He was to prepare the way for the Messiah. So when the time came for Jesus to begin His ministry, John willingly directed others to Him and allowed his own powerful ministry to take a backseat to Jesus.

John was Jesus' relative, and his own birth, like Jesus', was foretold by the angel Gabriel (Luke 1). John grew up to be a prophet, living in the desert and dressing in clothing similar to Elijah's (2 Kings 1:8; Matthew 3:4). He preached the message, "Repent, for the kingdom of heaven has come near"—the same message Jesus would later preach (Matthew 4:17) after John baptized Him. Jesus held John in very high esteem, declaring that no man has ever been greater than he (Matthew 11:11). John's ministry and his call for repentance were so widespread that years after his death he had followers as far away as Ephesus (Acts 19:1–5).

As great as John's ministry was, however, he always understood that his role was to point to One who was greater: Jesus. John knew that Jesus was so great in comparison to him that he was not even worthy to untie Jesus' sandals (Mark 1:7).

John met his death when he was thrown in prison for speaking out against Herod Antipas's marriage to his brother's wife. Herod's wife eventually asked for John's head on a platter, and Herod ordered that it be done.

INSIGHT: John modeled the attitude that all believers should follow as we point others to Jesus. We may be serving Christ in a way that is very powerful and beneficial to many people, but ultimately Jesus is greater than anything we are doing. The time may come for us to allow our ministry to be overshadowed or even replaced by other things Jesus is doing, and we should imitate John's example and willingly allow that to happen.

Artist Pieter Lastman avoids the usual supposition that JONAH was swallowed by a whale, showing us instead, as in the wording of the King James Bible, a "great fish."

# JONAH
## Reluctant Prophet to the People of Nineveh

[Jonah] prayed to the LORD, "Isn't this what I said, LORD, when I was still
at home? That is what I tried to forestall by fleeing to Tarshish. I knew
that you are a gracious and compassionate God, slow to anger
and abounding in love, a God who relents from sending calamity."

JONAH 4:2

From movies to books to workplace spats, it seems that revenge is in and mercy
is out. That was true for Jonah as well. Jonah was a prophet from Israel who was
called by God to preach to the people of Nineveh—the capital city of the mighty
Assyrian Empire. This great empire was threatening to swallow up tiny Israel
and everyone in it, and Jonah was not pleased about his new assignment.

So instead of heading for Nineveh, Jonah hopped on a slow boat to Tarshish—which was located in the opposite direction. But God cared too much about
both Jonah and the people of Nineveh to let him go without a fight. So the Lord
sent a storm that led the other sailors to throw Jonah overboard—then He sent
a fish to snatch Jonah from a watery grave. In God's grace, Jonah was given a
second chance to go to Nineveh to call the people to repent—and this time Jonah
took it.

For most people, that's where the story stops, but that's really only half the
story. The people of Nineveh did repent, and God, in keeping with His character,
relented from carrying out the destruction He had threatened for the city. Good
news, right? Not for Jonah. He was actually *angry* at God for being compassionate and sparing the city!

INSIGHT: How do you respond when you are threatened or even
hurt by others? Do you seek revenge? Do you pray for God to do
nasty things to your enemies? Jesus calls us to pray for our enemies
(Matthew 5:43–47). Since we have been spared eternal punishment for
our sins (Romans 6:23), how can we wish anything else for others?

Though Mary was His mother, God was the actual father of Jesus. But Mary's husband, JOSEPH, played the earthly role of father to the young Messiah.

# JOSEPH
## Earthly Father of Jesus

An angel of the Lord appeared to him in a dream and said, "Joseph
son of David, do not be afraid to take Mary home as your wife,
because what is conceived in her is from the Holy Spirit."
MATTHEW 1:20

Along with great pride, most new fathers feel some amount of anxiety over the
new responsibilities they face. But no one has ever really understood the burden
placed on Joseph's shoulders: raising the Son of God. Where's the manual for
that one? Who would you ask for advice?

Even before Jesus was born, however, Joseph had faced a great deal, and his
good character was already beginning to show. When he learned that his fiancée,
Mary, was pregnant with a child that wasn't his, he mercifully planned to divorce
her quietly and spare her public disgrace. Then an angel appeared to him in a
dream and told him that he should marry her—because the baby was conceived
by the Holy Spirit and would be the Savior of the world (Matthew 1:18–21).

When Mary gave birth to Jesus, Joseph watched, no doubt amazed, as people came from far and near to worship the baby as the divine King. Then an
angel appeared to him again and warned him to take his family to Egypt to avoid
being killed by King Herod. Later Joseph returned to his hometown of Nazareth,
where he continued to raise Jesus, the Savior of the world (Matthew 2).

When Jesus was twelve, Joseph and Mary were reminded again of Jesus' true
identity when they found Him in the temple astounding the teachers with His
questions. Jesus reminded them that the temple was His true Father's house, so
it should be no surprise that He would be there (Luke 2:40–52).

INFORMATION: Joseph was apparently a carpenter by trade
(Matthew 13:55), and he must have passed these skills on to Jesus
as well, because Jesus is also referred to as a carpenter in one of the
Gospels (Mark 6:3).

A modern artist's impression of JOSEPH, the Hebrew slave turned second-in-command of all Egypt.

# JOSEPH
## Favorite Son of Jacob

But Joseph said to [his brothers], "Don't be afraid. Am I in the place of God?
You intended to harm me, but God intended it for good to accomplish
what is now being done, the saving of many lives."

GENESIS 50:19-20

Joseph was no victim. Though the Bible recounts episode after episode of wrongs being done to him, Joseph knew—or perhaps learned—that ultimately God was in charge of everything, and He was working all things together for the good of His people.

Joseph was the eleventh and favorite son of Jacob, and his favored status earned him resentment from his brothers, who eventually sold him as a slave to some merchants traveling to Egypt (Genesis 37). Once there, Joseph was sold to a royal official named Potiphar, who quickly recognized and benefited from Joseph's administrative gifts. Later Potiphar's wife falsely accused Joseph of assaulting her, and he was thrown into prison (Genesis 39).

While in prison, Joseph demonstrated the ability to interpret dreams, and he was brought before Pharaoh to explain some troubling dreams. Joseph correctly foretold a great famine that was going to come upon the whole world, so Pharaoh elevated him to second in command of the kingdom. The famine drove Joseph's brothers to Egypt for food as well, and after a series of interactions with them, Joseph revealed his identity to them (Genesis 40–45).

Joseph's brothers feared that he would seek revenge on them for selling him into slavery, but Joseph recognized that God was orchestrating the events of his life for the good of His people—and that he should not assume the role of God and repay his brothers for their wrongs against him (Genesis 50).

INSIGHT: When others commit wrongs against us and cause us hardship, it is understandable if we feel angry and desire that God bring justice to our situation. Ultimately, however, we should recognize that we are not really at their mercy but at the mercy of God, who loves us and is always working all things together for our good (Romans 8:28–29).

JOSHUA and Caleb were the only two spies who trusted God to give the "promised land" to Israel.

# JOSHUA
## Hebrew Military Leader

*"But charge Joshua, and encourage and strengthen him,
for he shall go over at the head of this people,
and he shall put them in possession of the land that you shall see."*
DEUTERONOMY 3:28 ESV

Moses led the people to the doorstep of the Promised Land, but Joshua helped the people walk through the door to conquer and settle the land. Though born a slave in Egypt, Joshua became Moses' primary aid and assistant (Exodus 24:13). During four decades at Moses' side, Joshua served in a variety of ways: He explored the Promised Land as one of the original twelve spies—along with Caleb, giving the only favorable report. He led the people into their first successful military battles (Exodus 17). And he joined Moses on the mountain of God (Exodus 24:13). After Moses' death and the completion of a forty-year apprenticeship, Joshua became the leader of the Hebrew people (Joshua 1–4).

Joshua assumed command during a time of military conquest. Having commissioned Moses to lead the people out of Egypt, God gave Joshua the job of leading them into Canaan. Under Joshua's leadership the people conquered Jericho, Ai, and the other people of the land (Joshua 12). After the dust of battle settled, Joshua divided and assigned the land as instructed by Moses (Joshua 13–19).

Even though Joshua's legacy primarily revolves around his military exploits, each of his conquests is marked by his faith in God. Urging the people to remember the teachings of Moses, Joshua constantly reminded them of God's presence and plan. He entered into battle with a dependence on God's strength. He lived out the exhortation he received at the beginning of his days in leadership: "Have I not commanded you? Be strong and courageous. Do not be frightened, and do not be dismayed, for the Lord your God is with you wherever you go" (Joshua 1:9 ESV).

INTERESTING. . . The name *Jesus* is derived from *Joshua*. Just as Joshua brought God's people into a physical Promised Land, so Jesus brings God's people into a spiritual Promised Land. Read more on this comparison and theme in Hebrews 4.

# JOSIAH
## The Reformer King

Josiah removed all the detestable idols from all the territory belonging to the Israelites, and he had all who were present in Israel serve the LORD their God. As long as he lived, they did not fail to follow the LORD, the God of their ancestors.
2 CHRONICLES 34:33-34

Imagine if the Bible disappeared—lost to history, with no surviving copies to be found. How would you know how to relate to God? How could you tell if you were obeying His will?

That was Judah's dilemma when Josiah took the throne at the age of eight. The Book of the Law had not been seen or read for generations—perhaps not since Hezekiah, the last good king of Judah (and Josiah's great-grandfather). Since then, Judah had sunk to new lows, particularly during the reign of Manasseh, who sacrificed humans and defiled the Jewish temple—only to be humiliated when the Assyrians took him prisoner.

Josiah had reigned for eight years when he decided to turn things around and follow God. Still a teenager, he implemented top-down reforms with zeal, obliterating pagan worship sites and repairing the temple. But with no Book of the Law to guide him, how would Josiah know what else needed to be done?

While cleaning the temple, a priest named Hilkiah rediscovered the Book of the Law. It was brought to Josiah and read aloud—but rather than celebrate, Josiah lamented. Its words were a painful reminder of how far the Israelites had wandered from God's ways. Even worse, the prophetess Huldah announced that it was too late for Judah to escape judgment. The only consolation for Josiah was that he would not live to see its demise.

This, however, did not discourage him from pursuing reform. He ordered the Book of the Law read aloud to the people, renewed the covenant with God, and reinstated the Jewish feast. Unfortunately, Josiah's untimely death in battle meant the throne passed to his son, Jehoahaz—who lasted just three months.

INSIGHT: Josiah followed God, even though he knew his country was doomed. His legacy of faithfulness is recorded for all to read in the scriptures. Josiah's life serves as a reminder of the value of unwavering devotion to God, even when the whole world seems to be moving in the opposite direction.

# JUDAH
## Fourth Son of Jacob

"The scepter will not depart from Judah, nor the ruler's staff from between his feet, until he to whom it belongs shall come and the obedience of the nations shall be his."
GENESIS 49:10

Judah is best known as the forefather of Israel's leading tribe. His family produced the royal bloodline that included both David and the Messiah. Judah enjoyed this position of honor because he was given his father's blessing—a blessing that, by custom, should have gone to the firstborn son.

Judah's path to preeminence was unlikely, to say the least. When his brothers decided to get rid of Joseph (the youngest member of their family), it was Judah who stepped in and persuaded them not to kill the boy. However, Judah's plan was little better than theirs—he suggested they sell Joseph into slavery instead.

Years later, Judah was given a once-in-a-lifetime opportunity for redemption. In Egypt to beg for food—and unaware that the official listening to their plea was in fact their long-lost brother, Joseph—the sons of Jacob found themselves in a crisis rapidly going from bad to worse. Joseph threatened to enslave the youngest son, Benjamin—at which point Judah intervened, offering to take Benjamin's place. The one who had sold Jacob's favorite son into slavery now volunteered to become a slave himself in order to spare another of Jacob's favorite sons.

This selfless act opened the door for Joseph's reconciliation with his brothers. More important, Judah demonstrated an integrity that his older brothers failed to match. When their aged father gathered his sons for one last blessing, it was Judah who received the blessing of the firstborn—not Reuben, Simeon, or Levi.

Judah's privileged position suggests that character matters more than birth order.

INTERESTING. . . Judah's story was not without its own embarrassment. He once slept with a prostitute who turned out to be his deceased sons' widow, Tamar. After his first two sons had died, Judah promised to give Tamar to his youngest son, Shelah. Judah, however, reneged on his promise and ended up impregnating his own daughter-in-law without even realizing who she was (see Genesis 38).

JUDAS ISCARIOT, as portrayed by a nineteenth-century actor in Oberammergau, Germany's famous passion play.

# JUDAS ISCARIOT
## Betrayer of Jesus

Then Jesus replied, "Have I not chosen you, the Twelve? Yet one of you
is a devil!" (He meant Judas, the son of Simon Iscariot, who,
though one of the Twelve, was later to betray him.)

JOHN 6:70-71

Scholars have long debated the real reason for Judas's betrayal of Jesus—suggesting as possible motives everything from greed to disillusionment.

Some believe Judas did it for the money. The blood payment, thirty pieces of silver, equaled four months' salary. According to John's Gospel, Judas was a thief who liked to "help himself" to money set aside to support Jesus' ministry (John 12:6).

Another theory notes that Judas was one of the only non-Galilean disciples. His surname, Iscariot, likely indicates his birthplace—Kerioth, a town in southern Judah. As an outsider, Judas may have felt alienated from the group.

Others insist that Judas was a Zealot, part of a Jewish guerilla movement bent on driving out the Romans by any means necessary. As it became clear that Jesus had no intention of waging a war, Judas grew disillusioned or fearful (or both) and began looking for a way out.

A variant on this theory suggests that Judas didn't mean to betray Jesus at all—that Judas was merely trying to force His hand, convinced Jesus would give the call to arms once He was confronted in the garden of Gethsemane.

Still others chalk it up to demonic possession, noting—as Luke does—that "Satan entered Judas" shortly before the betrayal (Luke 22:3) and leaving it at that.

Whatever the real reason (or reasons), it is clear that Judas did not see the world as Jesus did. In one of the only stories to mention Judas outside of his betrayal, he scoffed at the so-called waste of expensive perfume by the woman from Bethany (see John 12:1–11). Jesus saw the woman's gift as an act of devotion, preparing Him for His impending death and burial. Judas only saw money being poured down the drain—money he wanted for himself. Judas demonstrated greed, hypocrisy, and an unwillingness to associate himself with Jesus' death—values that have no place in God's kingdom.

INTERESTING. . .The disciples' first order of business after Jesus'
ascension was replacing Judas. In the book of Acts, Luke chose not to
spare his readers the grisly details of Judas's suicide, noting that the
betrayer's "body burst open and all his intestines spilled out" (Acts 1:18).

# JUDE
## Half Brother of Jesus

Keep yourselves in God's love as you wait for the mercy of our Lord Jesus
Christ to bring you to eternal life.
JUDE 21

Jude is a relatively obscure figure in the New Testament—which is quite remarkable, given his family connection to the Messiah.

In all likelihood, Jude was the half brother of Jesus, yet he made no effort to peddle his relationship in order to gain attention or influence. In his letter to fellow believers, Jude introduced himself, not as the brother of Jesus, but as the "brother of James," another of Jesus' half brothers. Jude did not even claim the privileged title of "apostle," instead referring to himself as a mere "servant of Jesus Christ" (Jude 1).

Jude's humility and lack of ambition can be seen in his purpose for writing the New Testament letter that bears his name. Jude set aside his own agenda—that is, his desire to write about "the salvation we share" (Jude 3)—in order to address more pressing matters that were affecting his audience.

Apparently, false teachers were infiltrating the church, telling all who would listen that once saved by God, they could live however they wanted—because they were already covered by grace. Jude responded with a brief history lesson, reminding believers that even though God once saved the Hebrews from slavery in Egypt, He still punished those who rebelled against Him in the wilderness—those who, according to Jude, "did not believe" (Jude 5).

Jude regarded these false teachers as a threat to the very gospel his half brother had come to proclaim. He described them as "blemishes at your love feasts," "clouds without rain," and "twice dead" (Jude 12). Yet, despite the urgency of his message, Jude did not resort to using his connection to Jesus as a club with which to beat his audience into submission. Instead, he relied entirely on the truth and power of what he called the "most holy faith" (Jude 20).

INTERESTING. . . Jude can be found in the Gospels—but you have to look closely. In Mark 6:3, people respond to Jesus' teaching in His hometown, Nazareth, by asking, "Isn't this Mary's son and the brother of James, Joseph, Judas and Simon?" Judas is a variant of the name Jude—and most likely a reference to the New Testament author.

# KETURAH
## Abraham's Second Wife

Abraham left everything he owned to Isaac. But while he was still living, he gave gifts to the sons of his concubines and sent them away from his son Isaac.
GENESIS 25:5-6

Keturah's descendants were proof that blood is not necessarily thicker than water. Genesis provides no background on Keturah—she is simply (and quickly) introduced as Abraham's second wife. They married some time after Sarah died and Abraham's son Isaac had begun his new life with his bride, Rebekah. In one of the Bible's most extensive genealogies, the chronicler does not even acknowledge Keturah as a full-fledged wife—merely as "Abraham's concubine" (1 Chronicles 1:32).

Nevertheless, Keturah bore Abraham six sons: Zimran, Jokshan, Medan, Midian, Ishbak, and Shuah. Keturah's sons, however, did not share in Abraham's inheritance—everything went to Isaac. Shortly before he died, Abraham sent Keturah's sons away, though he did not dismiss them empty-handed. Abraham may well have felt fatherly affection for the children he had with Keturah, prompting him to give each child an unspecified gift. Still, he wanted to put some distance between them and his beloved son Isaac.

That distance would not prevent their stories from interweaving—sometimes with explosive results. Keturah's sons settled in Arabia, where one of them became the ancestor of the Midianites. It was Midianite merchants who sold Abraham's great-grandson Joseph into slavery in Egypt. Later Moses fled to Midian, where he married the daughter of a Midianite priest named Jethro. The Midianites conspired with Moab to curse the Hebrews as they entered the Promised Land—and during the time of Gideon, the Midianites were responsible for repeated incursions into Hebrew territory.

INSIGHT: Minor character though she was, Keturah played an important role in fulfilling God's covenant with Abraham. God did not just promise to make Abraham into a "great nation" (Genesis 12:2); He also swore that Abraham would become the father of "many nations" (Genesis 17:4). This promise was fulfilled, in part, through Keturah's offspring.

# LABAN
## Jacob's Deceitful Father-in-Law

Moreover, Jacob deceived Laban the Aramean
by not telling him he was running away.
GENESIS 31:20

Laban spent the better part of twenty years trying to outwit his son-in-law Jacob—a man whose name was a Hebrew idiom for "the deceiver."

Laban had a natural talent for shrewdness. Long before Jacob was born, his grandfather Abraham sent a servant in search of a wife for Isaac. When the servant happened upon Laban's sister and presented her with fine jewelry, Laban took one look, saw his opportunity, and adopted the persona of an accommodating host. Laban helped to arrange his sister's marriage and received some "costly gifts" for doing so (Genesis 24:53).

Laban's cunning reached new heights when Jacob arrived, shortly after stealing the birthright from his brother Esau. Jacob fell in love with Laban's youngest daughter, Rachel, and offered to serve Laban for seven years in exchange for Rachel's hand in marriage. On the wedding night, Laban managed to switch brides—Jacob awoke the next morning to see Jacob's oldest daughter, Leah, not Rachel, lying next to him! Laban agreed to let Jacob marry Rachel, too, but only after extracting the promise of another seven years of labor.

Ultimately, however, Laban's life is a reminder that people tend to reap what they sow. Not only did the con man get conned in the end, but also Laban's daughter Rachel inherited her father's talent for deception and turned it against him.

Laban got years of cheap labor out of Jacob (and changed his wages several times, according to Jacob), but Jacob managed to enrich himself at Laban's expense.

INTERESTING. . . Laban was not just Jacob's father-in-law; he was also Jacob's uncle. Laban's sister Rebekah was Jacob's mother. In other words, Leah and Rachel were Jacob's cousins. Such incestuous marriages (in the modern view) were not unheard of in the ancient Near East.

Deceivers, side-by-side—LABAN and his son-in-law Jacob. In the painting, Laban is looking for his household idols, stolen by his daughter Rachel—who adds her own deception to the family legacy.

# LAZARUS
## Raised from the Dead

When he had said this, Jesus called in a loud voice, "Lazarus, come out!"
JOHN 11:43

Lazarus and Jesus were so close that names did not need to be mentioned when word reached Jesus that His friend was ill. He was simply told, "The one you love is sick" (John 11:3).

Lazarus and his sisters, Mary and Martha, probably belonged to a wealthy family, as evidenced by the expensive perfume Mary poured on Jesus' feet after He raised Lazarus from the dead. It is possible the three siblings supported Jesus' ministry financially.

In any case, a deep bond existed between Lazarus and Jesus—so much so that Jesus willingly risked His life returning to Judea in order to "wake him up" (John 11:11). By the time Jesus arrived, however, Lazarus was unquestionably dead. John notes that Lazarus had been in the grave four days, which was significant because of the widely held Jewish belief that the soul departed the body three days after death. In other words, people might have accepted the possibility that Lazarus could be raised within the first three days—that is, before he was truly, irreversibly dead, but any hope of resurrection evaporated after the fourth day.

Jesus, however, was undeterred.

Led to the tomb where Lazarus was buried, He became deeply troubled at the sight of Lazarus's sisters grieving—and almost certainly by His own grief as well. Jesus ordered Lazarus to come out of his tomb, and to the crowd's amazement, he obeyed.

No one knows how long Lazarus lived after being brought back to life, but this miracle set in motion the events that led to Jesus' own death and resurrection. Incensed at Jesus' growing popularity, the Pharisees decided the time had come to put Jesus to death.

INSIGHT: One thing is known about Lazarus's post-resurrection life: Like Jesus, he became the target of an assassination plot. As far as the religious leaders were concerned, a living and breathing Lazarus was almost as great a threat to their authority as the One who had raised him. Lazarus's story, then, is a picture of the cost of following Jesus. With new life comes new risk—and new opportunity to sacrifice all for Christ.

# LEVI
## Jacob's Son

"Simeon and Levi are brothers—their swords are weapons of violence."
GENESIS 49:5

Levi, Jacob and Leah's third son, brutally demonstrated his skill with a sword when he and his brother Simeon avenged their sister Dinah.

Dinah had been raped by a local Canaanite named Shechem. When Shechem and his father, Hamor, arrived to propose a marriage uniting the two families (Shechem was enamored with Dinah), Jacob's sons devised a cunning plan for vengeance. As the defining mark of God's covenant with Abraham, they insisted Shechem and all those affiliated with him be circumcised if they wanted to form a union with Jacob's family. Hamor and Shechem believed this was an opportunity to enrich themselves by absorbing Jacob's family and its wealth into their own—so they hastily agreed.

While Hamor and his men were recovering from their painful surgeries, Jacob's sons swooped down on their settlement. Levi, with his brother Simeon, led the charge, killing all the men of the town, while their brothers plundered the place and took the women and children for themselves.

On his deathbed years later, Jacob recalled Levi's propensity for violence, criticizing his anger, fury, and cruelty (see Genesis 49:5–7). As punishment for Levi's aggression, Jacob warned that his descendants would have no territory to call their own—rather, they would be scattered throughout the Promised Land.

Jacob's promise came true—though God turned it into more of a blessing than a curse. In the wilderness, the descendants of Levi rallied to Moses after the Israelites worshipped the golden calf. As a reward, Moses promised the Levites they would be "set apart" for God (Exodus 32:29). Both promises came true: The Levites did not receive a tribal inheritance, but as priests to the nation, they served as mediators between God and His people.

INFORMATION: The book of Leviticus, which contains the priestly law, is named for Levi's descendants.

# LOIS
## Timothy's Grandmother

I have been reminded of your sincere faith,
which first lived in your grandmother Lois and in your mother
Eunice and, I am persuaded, now lives in you also.

2 TIMOTHY 1:5

Lois is the first of three generations of unlikely believers. Paul paid tribute to her and (presumably) her daughter Eunice in a letter to his young protégé Timothy.

Paul first arrived in Lystra, Lois's hometown, during his first missionary journey. While there, Paul healed a man who was unable to walk from birth, only to be mistaken as the incarnation of the Greek god Hermes. Subsequently, Paul was stoned by an angry mob and left for dead. Apparently the visit wasn't a total disaster, though. By the time he returned on his second missionary journey, Paul found at least three believers: Timothy, his mother, Eunice, and his grandmother Lois.

Little is known about Lois, the family matriarch. Her daughter Eunice had married a Greek, which may have generated social friction between the family and the rest of the Jewish community in Lystra. (Mixed marriages with pagans were roundly criticized in the Old Testament. Ezra, for example, was "appalled" at word that some of the returning exiles had taken Gentile spouses—see Ezra 9:4.)

In any case, Lois's grandson Timothy was a paradox—steeped in the Old Testament from a young age, no doubt thanks to Lois and Eunice, yet never circumcised, perhaps due to the influence of his Greek father. In the end, it was Lois's influence that prevailed, leaving a lasting mark on Timothy. Paul, impressed by Timothy's devotion to Christ, became his mentor and eventually made him pastor of the church at Ephesus.

INSIGHT: Lois serves as a reminder that it is not necessary to play a leading role in order to have a lasting impact. Mentioned by name just once in the Bible, Lois was nevertheless vital in shaping the character and convictions of one of the early church's most influential young pastors. Those who serve God behind the scenes play no less an important role than those who serve for all to see.

LOT and his family, guided by an angel, prepare to leave Sodom in a painting by the Dutch master Peter Paul Rubens.

# LOT
## Abraham's Nephew

And if he rescued Lot, a righteous man, who was distressed by the depraved conduct of the lawless. . .then the Lord knows how to rescue the godly from trials.

2 PETER 2:7, 9

*Righteous* is not the first word that usually comes to mind when the subject is a man named Lot.

Lot accompanied Abraham to the Promised Land. Once there, tensions grew as he and Abraham tried to tend their flocks on limited resources in a land that did not fully belong to them. Abraham proposed they go their separate ways and magnanimously gave Lot the choice of which direction to take—especially remarkable in a culture where the family patriarch's word was final. Lot chose what appeared to be the best land and eventually set aside the nomadic life in order to settle in one of the nearby cities, Sodom.

Lot seemed to resist the worst of Sodom's vice, which may explain why he was considered "righteous." He alone offered hospitality to the angelic visitors. Honor-bound to protect his guests, he attempted to spare them from the angry mob—even though the offer of his own daughters understandably strikes modern readers as detestable. Lot even tried to warn his extended family of God's impending judgment.

His family, however, did not fare as well. Lot's wife ignored the angels' command, looked back on the city, and died as they fled. His daughters, convinced they had no hope of finding husbands, slept with Lot in order to become pregnant.

Nevertheless, Peter held Lot as an example of righteousness—proof that God can deliver His people from difficulty. Lot also benefited from Abraham's superior righteousness. The writer of Genesis sums up the story of Sodom by noting that God "remembered Abraham, and he brought Lot out of the catastrophe" (Genesis 19:29).

INSIGHT: Lot is famous for choosing what he considered the best land, while leaving his uncle to tend his flocks in a less hospitable environment. Lot's choice, however, proved disastrous for him and his family, while Abraham was rewarded with "offspring like the dust of the earth" (Genesis 13:16). The difference between the two came down to faith. Lot based his choice on what he could see, while Abraham trusted in what he could not see.

The Gentile physician LUKE is sometimes pictured with an ox, a symbol of sacrifice, service, and strength—themes in his Gospel of Luke.

# LUKE
## Paul's Traveling Companion

With this in mind, since I myself have carefully investigated everything from the beginning, I too decided to write an orderly account for you, most excellent Theophilus, so that you may know the certainty of the things you have been taught.

LUKE 1:3-4

Surprisingly little is known about the man who wrote a quarter of the New Testament. What is known, however, is that Luke brought his unique set of skills to bear—including his expertise as a physician and his keen eye for detail—in writing an account of the life of Jesus and the early church.

Luke was not an eyewitness to Jesus' ministry. At the beginning of his Gospel, he described himself as a researcher who "carefully investigated everything" (Luke 1:3). Of the four Gospels, Luke's has the most in common with classical Greek literature—its sophisticated style of writing reflects favorably on the author's education.

However, Luke was no ivory tower academic, writing about things from afar. Luke was friends with the apostle Paul. Beginning with Paul's second missionary journey, the two men became traveling companions. (Notice Luke's use of the pronoun *we* starting in Acts 16:10.) As such, Luke witnessed firsthand many of the incidents recorded in the book of Acts. He may well have suffered imprisonment and persecution alongside Paul. He was there with Paul when a ship bound for Crete broke apart, nearly drowning everyone on board. Some believe he put his medical training to use at key moments, such as when Paul was bitten by a snake on the island of Malta.

Luke was part doctor, part historian, and part adventurer—but most of all, he was a dedicated, articulate, compelling advocate for the good news of Jesus Christ.

INTERESTING. . . Luke is probably the only Gentile author represented in the New Testament. Near the end of his letter to the Colossians, Paul included Luke in a list of Gentile companions who sent their greetings to the believers in Colosse (see Colossians 4:14).

LYDIA, a "dealer in purple cloth," was the first Christian convert in Europe.

# LYDIA

## First Believer from Paul's Ministry in Europe

One of those listening was a woman from the city of Thyatira named Lydia,
a dealer in purple cloth. She was a worshiper of God. The Lord
opened her heart to respond to Paul's message.

ACTS 16:14

Lydia has the great distinction of being the first person in Europe to respond to Paul's presentation of the gospel.

Paul met Lydia in the city of Philippi while he was on his second missionary journey. He had just sailed from the city of Troas in Asia Minor to the port city of Neapolis, which is near Philippi in Macedonia (northern Greece). There must not have been very many Jews in Philippi, because Paul did not go to a synagogue on the Sabbath as he usually did. Instead, he went to a nearby riverbank, where any Jews who did live there would likely have met for prayer.

There he found several women, including Lydia, a "worshiper of God," which usually meant a Gentile convert to Judaism. She was actually from the city of Thyatira in Asia Minor and was likely wealthy, since she was a dealer in purple cloth. When Paul began to speak to the women about the gospel, Lydia responded, became a believer, and was baptized. Later she invited Paul and his companions to stay with her family. Still later, after Paul and Silas were released from prison, they returned to Lydia's house, encouraged the fledgling church that was started there, and then left to travel farther throughout Macedonia.

INFORMATION: By the time of Paul, Philippi, while not large, was a significant Roman city—home to many retired Roman soldiers and granted exemption from most taxes.

# MALCHUS
## Caiaphas's Servant

"Put your sword back in its place," Jesus said to him,
"for all who draw the sword will die by the sword."
MATTHEW 26:52

Malchus was a personal servant to Caiaphas, the high priest who led the conspiracy to have Jesus arrested and killed. Probably on Caiaphas's orders, Malchus accompanied Judas and the party seeking to arrest Jesus while He prayed in the Garden of Gethsemane. As the situation threatened to explode into chaos, Malchus found himself very much in the wrong place at the wrong time.

Cornered, Jesus' disciples watched the horrifying scene unfold—one, however, decided to act. Peter unsheathed a sword and swung, severing Malchus's ear. It may have been the combination of instinct and adrenaline that drove Peter's hand. Or it may have been his failure to understand the true nature and purpose of Jesus' ministry. As Malchus writhed in pain, Jesus rebuked his attacker, warning Peter that "all who draw the sword will die by the sword" (Matthew 26:52).

Determined that no blood but His own be shed on His account, Jesus somehow managed to reach Malchus and heal his injury before being dragged away by the temple guard. Malchus, then, provided the object lesson in one last teaching to the disciples before Jesus' crucifixion—one final reminder that His kingdom would not come by force or be spread by the sword. What happened to Malchus after this incident—and whether he returned to his master, the man who plotted Jesus' murder—is unknown.

INTERESTING. . . While uncertain, the attack on Malchus may have had hidden significance. Assuming Malchus was a Levite, like his master and all who belonged to the priestly class, a defect like the loss of an ear would have rendered him unclean according to the Law of Moses. Malchus would have been forbidden from going anywhere near the temple (see Leviticus 21). If this was the case, then Jesus not only restored Malchus's ear—He restored his livelihood.

In the confusion over the arrest of Jesus, Peter slashes at MALCHUS. The high priest's servant will lose an ear in the confrontation—but have it quickly restored by Jesus.

# MANASSEH
## King of Judah

Moreover, Manasseh also shed so much innocent blood
that he filled Jerusalem from end to end.
2 KINGS 21:16

Long life and a long reign were often taken as signs of God's favor. But Judah's longest-reigning monarch proved the exception. During his fifty-five-year reign, Manasseh led his people into shocking new depths of idolatry and immorality.

Ironically, Manasseh's father, Hezekiah, was one of Judah's great reformers—but Manasseh was determined to restore Judah's idolatry. He embraced an "all of the above" approach to religion—adopting the Baal cult of the Canaanites, who once occupied the Promised Land, borrowing astrology from the Babylonians, who would crush Jerusalem not one hundred years later, and reviving nature worship from the depths of early humanity. But for the writers of Kings and Chronicles, two acts in particular confirmed Manasseh's place as an object of revulsion: human sacrifice and the desecration of God's temple.

Despite his long rule, Manasseh appears to have been no more than a client king, subject to the Assyrian Empire, the reigning superpower of the day. An ancient artifact called the Prism of Ashurbanipal identifies Manasseh as one of nearly two dozen regional kings who paid tribute to Assyria. At one point, Manasseh was dragged to Babylon on orders from the Assyrian king, something the chronicler took as proof of God's displeasure (see 2 Chronicles 33:10–13).

This humiliation proved to be a pivotal moment for Manasseh. Upon returning to Jerusalem, Manasseh removed pagan objects from the temple grounds and restored the altar by making fellowship and thank offerings to God. Manasseh stopped short of purging the whole country of its idolatry, however. Nonetheless, God was moved by Manasseh's willingness to humble himself.

INTERESTING. . . The author of 2 Chronicles reveals that Manasseh sacrificed humans "in the fire in the Valley of Ben Hinnom" (2 Chronicles 33:6). This valley, just outside Jerusalem, was so detestable that it became the primary image for hell in Jewish thought. The word *gehenna*, which Jesus used frequently for hell (see, for example, Matthew 5:22), came from the Hebrew name for this valley where Manasseh sacrificed his own son.

# MANOAH
## Samson's Father

And the Lord did an amazing thing while Manoah and his wife watched:
As the flame blazed up from the altar toward heaven, the angel of the Lord
ascended in the flame.

JUDGES 13:19-20

Any parent who watches a child turn out differently from what was hoped can appreciate the story of Manoah.

Manoah and his wife suffered two kinds of hardship: they lived under the yoke of the Philistines and they were childless. Still, when the angel of the Lord told Manoah's wife that she was going to bear a son who would deliver His people from the hated Philistines, Manoah found the courage to believe the impossible. He prayed for God to send the mysterious visitor once more—not because he didn't trust his wife, but because he wanted to know how they should raise their promised son.

Manoah's faith was rewarded when the visitor returned to the awestruck couple. While the angel refused Manoah's hospitality—he had offered to prepare a young goat, no small delicacy in those days—he invited Manoah to make a burnt offering to God. Manoah did so, and while he and his wife watched, the angel rode the flame back to heaven. Only then did they realize that God Himself had visited them. Convinced they were about to die, Manoah needed his wife's reassurance that God would not accept their offering and promise them a son only to kill them.

Nevertheless, Manoah was destined to experience great anguish on account of the son that God provided. That son, Samson, was to be one of Israel's great deliverers—unfortunately, he fell far short of the godly example set by his parents. Much to their distress, Samson took a pagan wife from their enemies, the Philistines. It is not known whether Manoah lived to see his son's demise, but he certainly watched Samson take those first fateful steps toward personal destruction.

INSIGHT: For someone who lived in a patriarchal culture (and one where barren women were especially despised), Manoah demonstrated a surprising degree of respect for his wife. He took her word when she told him of the angelic visitation. Also, it was Manoah's wife who had the better understanding of things when the angel of the Lord disappeared in the flames of the couple's burnt offering.

A sixteenth-century oil painting of MARK the evangelist. Many believe an unnamed man at the arrest of Jesus, referred to in Mark 14, is Mark himself: "A young man, wearing nothing but a linen garment, was following Jesus. When they seized him, he fled naked, leaving his garment behind" (verses 51–52).

# MARK
## Coworker of Paul and Gospel Writer

Luke alone is with me. Get Mark and bring him with you,
for he is very useful to me for ministry.
2 TIMOTHY 4:11 ESV

Mark (also called John Mark) is a shining example of the power of God to re-deem failed disciples. If you read only the book of Acts, you might come away thinking that Mark was simply another sad example of an unfaithful believer gone astray, and that was the end of the story. Not true.

Mark was a relative of Barnabas (Colossians 4:10) and was among the first believers in the early church. He accompanied Paul and Barnabas on their first missionary journey (Acts 13:5), but it seems that when things got rough, Mark decided to pack up and head home to Jerusalem (Acts 13:13; 15:37–38). Later, when Paul and Barnabas were considering making a second missionary journey, Paul was firmly decided that Mark should not be allowed to come (Acts 15:39).

Fortunately, the story doesn't end there. Barnabas, the great encourager, took Mark along to Cyprus, perhaps on a second missionary trip through Barnabas's home region (Acts 15:39). Apparently this second opportunity for Mark to show himself faithful paid off, because by the time Paul wrote Colossians and Phile-mon, he was referring to Mark as his fellow worker (Colossians 4:10; Philemon 24). Paul's great regard for Mark comes through most clearly late in his life in his second letter to Timothy, where Paul describes Mark as helpful in the ministry (2 Timothy 4:11). Even Peter later referred to Mark as a son (1 Peter 5:13).

INTERESTING. . . Church tradition says that Mark composed the second Gospel from Peter's sermons. In the first half of the second century, an early church leader named Papias wrote, "Mark, having become the interpreter of Peter, wrote down accurately whatsoever he remembered. It was not, however, in exact order that he related the sayings or deeds of Christ. For he neither heard the Lord nor accompanied Him. But afterwards, as I said, he accompanied Peter, who accommodated his instructions to the necessities [of his hearers]."

MARTHA and Mary provide a real-life example of the debate over which is more important in Christian life, works or faith.

# MARTHA
## Sister of Mary and Lazarus

"Martha, Martha," the Lord answered, "you are worried and upset about many things, but few things are needed—or indeed only one. Mary has chosen what is better, and it will not be taken away from her."

It seems like it's the same every holiday. We have good intentions of reflecting on the true meaning of the special day and focusing on Jesus, but inevitably we can never seem to fit this in amid all the busyness of preparing food or visiting family or buying gifts or whatever. We are too much like Martha and not enough like her sister, Mary.

Martha was the sister of Mary and Lazarus. The three of them lived near Jerusalem in a small village named Bethany. Because of their friendship with Jesus and their proximity to the holy city, Jesus seemed to regularly stay with them while he was in the area.

On one of these visits, Martha worked hard at serving Jesus and grew indignant when her sister, Mary, sat beside Jesus rather than help with the preparations. Jesus gently rebuked Martha instead, telling her that she was not choosing the most important thing: being in Jesus' presence.

Martha's busy nature can be seen again at a meal given in Jesus' honor in their home. Martha served while Lazarus reclined and ate with the other guests at the dinner. Mary later demonstrated her love for Jesus by pouring perfume on Jesus' feet and wiping His feet with her hair.

INSIGHT: Though we should be careful not to write Martha off completely as someone only consumed with daily chores and uninterested in spending time with Jesus, she does stand as a bit of a negative example to believers today. We should make sure that we are always keeping the main thing the main thing: spending time with Jesus and enjoying Him.

This stained glass image of MARY with the baby Jesus reminds us that she was still just a girl when God entrusted her with the job of being mother to His Son.

# MARY
## Mother of Jesus

But the angel said to her, "Do not be afraid, Mary; you have found favor with God. You will conceive and give birth to a son, and you are to call him Jesus."

LUKE 1:30-31

Mary is, of course, best known as the virgin who gave birth to the Messiah—one of the most celebrated miracles in the Bible. But the New Testament also portrays Mary as a refreshingly human figure. In the Gospels, she is often characterized by her motherly concern for her son.

Twelve years after Jesus' miraculous birth, He accompanied His parents and their relatives and friends to Jerusalem for the Passover. When the time came to return home, Jesus lagged behind, wanting to spend more time among the rabbis in the temple. After three days of panicked searching, Mary and Joseph finally caught up with their son. The relief was obvious in Mary's words: "Son, why have you treated us like this? Your father and I have been anxiously searching for you" (Luke 2:48).

Years later, as Jesus began drawing large crowds—and as opposition started to form in some corners—Mary and her sons made a thirty-mile journey, intending to "take charge of him" (Mark 3:21). In all likelihood, Mary was concerned for Jesus' well-being; she simply wanted to protect her son from the ever-growing (and, no doubt, ever more demanding) crowds, not to mention the murmuring religious authorities who accused Jesus of being demon-possessed.

The Gospel of John provides yet another fleeting glimpse of Mary—this time at the foot of her son's cross. In the midst of His agony, Jesus spoke to His mother one last time. The sheer courage it must have taken to witness her son's execution is astounding. One of Jesus' final acts before giving up His spirit was entrusting His mother to the care of His most beloved disciple, John (John 19:26–27). Even at the climax of redemptive history, Jesus paused to make sure the mother who had loved Him so well was cared for.

INSIGHT: The crucifixion was not the first time Mary demonstrated extraordinary courage. Submitting herself to God's plan meant risking years of scorn—and perhaps worse. In all likelihood, most would have scoffed at her account of the angelic visitation and miraculous conception. What's more, the Mosaic law stated that a betrothed virgin who slept with another man was to be stoned. Mary, however, demonstrated great trust in God's ability to protect her.

At the Basilica of St. John Lateran in Rome, **MATTHEW** is depicted holding a book. The book probably represents the Bible (which wouldn't have been compiled in Matthew's lifetime), but in his pre-evangelistic days it might just as well have been a tax ledger.

# MATTHEW
## Tax Collector Turned Disciple

As Jesus went on from there, he saw a man named Matthew sitting at the tax collector's booth. "Follow me," he told him, and Matthew got up and followed him.

MATTHEW 9:9

Matthew sat at the crossroads of commerce. His tax collector's booth in Capernaum probably looked out on the Via Maris, one of the most important trading routes in the Roman Empire.

Local tax collectors were employed by the empire to keep Rome's coffers filled. They had a reputation for charging more than even Rome demanded and pocketing the extra—a habit that did not win many friends in occupied territories such as Galilee. In the ancient Jewish world, a tax collector's word was of no value in court, his presence was unwelcome at the synagogue, and even his own family might disown him.

Few would have approached Matthew's collection booth willingly—yet Jesus did. To some, it may seem strange that Matthew left behind a lucrative trade in order to wander the countryside with an itinerant preacher. Jesus, however, may have been one of the only people to offer Matthew an invitation of any kind. He may have been the first to look into Matthew's eyes—the eyes of one who, according to popular wisdom, should have been His enemy—and see a human being created in the image of God.

In that moment, Matthew left the crossroads of commerce to walk the crossroads of history. Not only did he accept Jesus' invitation—and extend one of his own, inviting Jesus to dinner—Matthew authored the Gospel that bears his name. Matthew wrote his account primarily for a Jewish audience—for the very people who had once despised him.

INSIGHT: Matthew's dinner party caused great controversy among the religious leaders, mainly because the guest list contained so many tax collectors and "sinners"—in other words, people who deliberately violated God's law. The religious authorities were offended because fellowship with sinners was believed to contaminate—and in the ancient world, one of the most intimate forms of fellowship was sharing a meal. Jesus' response revealed that where others saw potential for contamination, Jesus saw an opportunity to bring healing and wholeness.

MATTHIAS, chosen by lot to replace the deceased apostle Judas Iscariot, holds a square in this fresco from the 1700s. He is considered a patron saint of carpenters in some Christian traditions.

# MATTHIAS
## Disciple Chosen to Replace Judas Iscariot

Then they cast lots, and the lot fell to Matthias;
so he was added to the eleven apostles.

ACTS 1:26

What if, after all the primaries and campaign speeches, the president of the United States was to be decided by a coin toss?

You might ask, *How could the most powerful person in the world be chosen by such a random process?* Yet that is similar to the process used to decide who would fill one of the most important offices in the history of the world—the twelfth apostle of Jesus Christ.

While Jesus was ministering throughout Israel, He gathered many followers who had varying levels of commitment. Some belonged simply to the thousands that came and went. Others belonged to a group of seventy-two that were sent out by Jesus to minister to people (Luke 10:1, 17). Still others belonged to an inner circle of twelve who followed Jesus almost constantly and were privy to most of his teaching and deeds (Mark 3:16–19).

When Judas Iscariot, one of the Twelve, committed suicide after betraying Jesus to death, the eleven remaining disciples recognized the need to fill Judas's role as a witness to Christ. They stipulated that any candidates would need to have been with Jesus from the very beginning of His ministry.

After narrowing the candidates down to two men—Matthias and Joseph—the disciples "cast lots," meaning they used some process such as throwing dice or drawing straws, to make the final selection. In this way, they handed the final decision over to God, who oversees even things that we regard as chance. The lot fell to Matthias, and he became the twelfth apostle (Acts 1:15–26).

INSIGHT: While it is tempting to see this passage as undermining the necessity of wisdom in making decisions, it is important to recognize that the disciples did not simply put a bunch of names in a hat and pick one out. They used their own discretion to narrow the number of candidates down to two fully qualified people, and then they handed the final choice over to God.

In an ancient mosaic, MELCHIZEDEK blesses Abraham "by God Most High" (Genesis 14:19) after Abraham's military victory over an alliance of regional kings.

# MELCHIZEDEK
## Priest-King of Jerusalem

The LORD has sworn and will not change his mind:
"You are a priest forever, in the order of Melchizedek."

PSALM 110:4

In Genesis, Melchizedek was an obscure priest—a minor figure in Abraham's narrative. But to the writer of Hebrews, Melchizedek was a forerunner of the Messiah Himself.

The Old Testament identifies Melchizedek as "king of Salem" and "priest of God Most High" (Genesis 14:18). *Salem* was a contraction of *Jerusalem*, the city that became capital of the Promised Land and home to God's temple. In other words, Melchizedek was a priest before there was even a priesthood—he was king of God's holy city long before it had a temple.

When Abraham defeated Kedorlaomer's forces and rescued his nephew Lot, Melchizedek met him with bread and wine and blessed him in the name of God Most High. Abraham, in turn, gave Melchizedek a tenth of the spoils from his victory—the first tithe recorded in scripture.

Centuries later, when the writer of Hebrews pressed his case that Jesus was the ultimate priest, he appealed to the example of Melchizedek. Skeptics might have claimed that Jesus could not be regarded as a priest, since He did not descend from the tribe of Levi. But Hebrews notes that long before there was a Levite priesthood, there was Melchizedek. Jesus, then, was a priest "in the order of Melchizedek" (Hebrews 7:11). Furthermore, by the time of the Levite priesthood, the roles of priest and king had been carefully separated, whereas Melchizedek was *both* priest and king. Once more the writer of Hebrews compared Jesus to Melchizedek, concluding that Jesus is the high priest "who sat down at the right hand of the throne of the Majesty in heaven" (Hebrews 8:1). Melchizedek's brief story served as a preview of what was to come in the person and work of Jesus Christ.

INTERESTING. . . The writer of Hebrews says that Melchizedek was "without father or mother, without genealogy" (Hebrews 7:3). Indeed, Melchizedek quickly appears and disappears from the biblical record—without any reference to his family. In an ancient source called the Tell el-Amarna Letters, a king of Urusalim (perhaps synonymous with Jerusalem) tells the ruler of Egypt, "Neither my father nor my mother set me in this place." Some believe this mysterious king to be Melchizedek.

METHUSELAH lived to the age of 969. This stained glass window is from England's Canterbury Cathedral.

# METHUSELAH
## World's Longest-Living Person

Altogether, Methuselah lived a total of 969 years, and then he died.

GENESIS 5:27

There is no biblical reference to Methuselah outside of three genealogical records. Yet he is well-known as the world's longest-living person, having survived, according to the Bible, for nearly a millennium.

The writer of Genesis recorded two family lines that descended from Adam and Eve. One was the family of Cain, the world's first murderer. The other was the family of Seth, to which Methuselah belonged. The two groups could not have been more different. Cain's family was industrious—playing musical instruments and working with metal—but it was also violent. Lamech, one of Cain's descendants, openly bragged about slaying two young men.

After chronicling Cain's descendants, the writer of Genesis notes that "at that time people began to call on the name of the LORD" (Genesis 4:26). With that, he launched into the account of the other family line—that of Seth. The most obvious characteristic of Seth's descendants was their propensity for long life spans. Five individuals mentioned, including Methuselah, exceeded nine hundred years. More important, however, this was the family that called upon God. Methuselah's father, Enoch, was the first man said to have "walked with God" (see Genesis 5:24). Methuselah's son, Lamech (no connection to the descendant of Cain), recognized God's role in their lives. And Methuselah's grandson, Noah, was found to be "blameless among the people of his time" (Genesis 6:9).

Perhaps even more remarkable than his age was the family to which Methuselah belonged—and their willingness to "call on the name of the Lord."

INTERESTING. . . Though Methuselah was history's longest-living person, the Bible records that he died the same year as the great flood of Noah's day. The Bible doesn't record if God graciously allowed him to die before the flood or if he was one of the wicked people who perished in the flood. No matter the final outcome of his life, Luke 3 records that Methuselah was one of the ancestors of Jesus Christ.

# MICAH
## Old Testament Prophet

"Micah of Moresheth prophesied in the days of Hezekiah. . . . Did Hezekiah king of Judah or anyone else in Judah put him to death? Did not Hezekiah fear the Lord and seek his favor? And did not the Lord relent. . .?"
JEREMIAH 26:18-19

Micah's listeners may have dismissed him as an outsider—a country simpleton. He was not from Jerusalem, after all—he lived in the rural foothills of southern Judah. Yet that did not stop Micah from delivering a forceful message aimed directly at the rampant corruption of Judah's elite.

His prophecy was relatively straightforward. According to Micah, it was not hard to figure out why God was angry with Judah. Her wealthy landowners had committed fraud and outright theft, taking people's farms and homes, depriving them of their livelihood and inheritance (Micah 2:1–2). The authorities were systematically subverting justice and oppressing the poor (Micah 3:1–9). Judah's merchants were cheating people with dishonest scales (Micah 6:11). Even the religious leaders did not escape God's wrath, according to Micah—they had turned the sacred ministry of teaching into a commercial venture, demanding a price for their services (Micah 3:11).

Micah—whose prophecy is often compared to that of his contemporary Isaiah—was forceful and impassioned. His writing bore the marks of a divine lawsuit: God was, in effect, taking His people to court over their abuses and injustices (see Micah 6:1–2). Micah predicted that both Israel and Judah would reap calamity for their sins. Samaria would fall first, but soon disaster would reach "even to the gate of Jerusalem" (Micah 1:12).

---

INSIGHT: For all of Micah's doom and gloom, he also promised hope—a time of restoration when God's people would return to Him and pursue peace instead of violence (see Micah 4–5). In fact, each of Micah's three oracles of judgment was followed by a promise of restoration.

# MICHAL
## Wife of King David

Saul sent men to David's house to watch it and to kill him in the morning. But Michal, David's wife, warned him, "If you don't run for your life tonight, tomorrow you'll be killed."

1 SAMUEL 19:11

Michal's story reads like something from an ancient soap opera: romance, intrigue, feuding families, and a politically motivated lover's triangle.

Michal was the youngest daughter of Saul. She fell in love with David at a time her father was looking for a way to have him killed. Sensing his opportunity, Saul promised Michal to David in exchange for killing one hundred Philistines. Surely it was a suicide mission—except that David managed to kill *two* hundred Philistines. Not only had Saul's plan failed, but also he was forced to watch his youngest daughter marry his enemy.

Saul schemed once more to take David's life, but Michal uncovered the plot and helped her husband escape. While David climbed out a window, Michal used a household idol to make it look like David was asleep in bed, underneath a garment (see 1 Samuel 19:11–16).

After David when into hiding, Saul gave Michal to a man named Paltiel—a deliberate insult, perhaps designed to weaken David's claim to the throne. After Saul died, David demanded that Michal be returned to him—much to Paltiel's chagrin.

Michal, too, may have resented being treated like a pawn in other people's plans. Or perhaps she simply did not share David's devotion to God. For whatever reason, the love between them seemed to grow cold after David became king. Michal even mocked David's exuberant display as the ark of the covenant was carried to Jerusalem. The Bible notes that Michal bore no children after her falling out with David—which may have been due to divine punishment or simply an indication that she no longer received David's favor or affection.

INSIGHT: Michal seemed to think that David's manner of worship was unbefitting the dignity of a king. David's response in 2 Samuel 6:21 ("I will celebrate before the Lord") serves as a reminder that pride and self-consciousness have no place in authentic worship—only a continual awareness that it is God whose pleasure we seek.

A Jew at heart, MORDECAI would probably have dressed in Persian clothes similar to these for his own safety.

# MORDECAI
## Queen Esther's Cousin

Mordecai the Jew was second in rank to King Xerxes, preeminent among the Jews, and held in high esteem by his many fellow Jews, because he worked for the good of his people and spoke up for the welfare of all the Jews.
ESTHER 10:3

In one of the Bible's most ironic plot twists, God used Mordecai, a man who tried to conceal his Jewish identity, to save the Jews from annihilation.

Mordecai settled in Susa (present-day Iran), where he enjoyed a successful livelihood at the city gates, a hub of commerce in the ancient world. The Bible portrays Mordecai as a conflicted figure. On the one hand, he demonstrated compassion and courage. Mordecai adopted his orphaned cousin Esther as his own daughter, and he uncovered a plot to assassinate the Persian king. On the other hand, Mordecai advanced his and Esther's fortunes primarily by concealing their Jewish ethnicity.

Mordecai found his nemesis in Haman, a royal official who probably descended from the Amalekites. The Jews and Amalekites had been enemies since the days of Sinai, when the Amalekites attacked the Jewish people following their escape from Egypt. When Mordecai refused to pay homage to Haman, the latter sought to finish the work his ancestors had begun in the wilderness years before.

Haman concocted a plan to exterminate the Jews—and personally arranged for Mordecai's execution. Just in time, however, the Persian king remembered Mordecai's lifesaving service to him. Just as Haman was preparing to ask the king's permission to execute Mordecai, the king ordered him to pay homage to Mordecai instead. Mordecai and Esther, their Jewish identity no longer a secret, were able to undermine Haman's plot to exterminate the Jews. Haman, meanwhile, ended up being impaled on the very pole he had set up for Mordecai's execution.

INSIGHT: Mordecai's story, told in the book of Esther, contains no mention of God. Indeed, Mordecai and Esther do not seem to have been particularly religious—Esther, for example, seemed to ignore Jewish dietary laws by freely eating from the king's table (see Esther 2:9). However, Mordecai's story is filled with a number of improbable "coincidences," which serve as a reminder that God is always at work, even when He cannot be seen.

MOSES displays God's laws, engraved in stone. The "stiff-necked people" of Israel managed to disobey several of the divine commands before he could even deliver them.

# MOSES
## Greatest Hebrew Prophet

Now the man Moses was very humble, more than
any man who was on the face of the earth.
NUMBERS 12:3 NASB

Arguably Israel's greatest prophet, Moses left behind one of the strongest leg-
acies in the Bible. As God's anointed leader, he led the people from Egypt to
the Promised Land, appointed priests and judges, created a place of worship,
delivered God's law, wrote the first five books of the Bible, and frequently interceded on behalf of the people. With this exceptional résumé, it's easy to envy a
character like Moses. Who wouldn't want to accomplish so much?

For Moses, though, the road to each accomplishment included a great many
difficult and rocky places as it twisted and turned. After becoming a fugitive from
Pharaoh's court, Moses scratched out a living in the desert of Midian as a shepherd for forty years (Exodus 3). Once commissioned by God, Moses then risked
his life by bringing bad news and judgment to Pharaoh (Exodus 4–12). And
though God gave him the task of confronting Pharaoh, Moses lacked natural
speaking ability and needed to rely on his brother, Aaron, to be his mouthpiece
(see Exodus 4:10).

Securing the freedom of the Hebrew people led to more difficulty for Moses. Instead of being heralded as a hero, he became the object of the Israelites'
complaints and rebellion (see examples in Exodus 15–17; Numbers 14, 16).

In spite of all his illustrious achievements as God's appointed leader, Moses
was not perfect. As a consequence for Moses' disobedience (Numbers 20), God
did not allow him to cross into the land. Instead, God graciously allowed Moses to
view the Promised Land that God had reserved for His people (Deuteronomy 34).

INFORMATION: Moses' life illustrated that the price of
leadership is often loneliness. During the difficult times of leading the
people through the wilderness, Moses faced opposition from those who
should have been his closest allies. Leadership is difficult and lonely
work. What leaders need to experience your support?

# NAAMAN
## Syrian Army Commander

Now Naaman was commander of the army of the king of Aram. . . .
He was a valiant soldier, but he had leprosy.
2 KINGS 5:1

Naaman was an unlikely candidate for healing by a prophet from Israel. After all, he commanded the army of Aram (present-day Syria), one of Israel's adversaries.

Unfortunately, Naaman's reputation for valor was not enough to protect him from one of the most shameful diseases the ancient world knew: leprosy. Ironically, though, it was one of Naaman's prisoners of war who pointed the way to his eventual cure—a young Jewish servant girl suggested that Naaman visit the prophet Elisha.

Naaman sought the blessing of his master, the king of Aram, who sent a hefty payment to Israel's king in order to procure Elisha's services. Naaman and his master seemed unaware that Israel's prophets answered not to human authorities, but to God alone. At first, the bribe had the opposite of the intended effect, alarming the Israelite king, who suspected the Arameans of trying to pick another fight. But Elisha intervened, sensing an opportunity to demonstrate the superiority of the one true God—both to Naaman and to Israel's own unbelieving king.

Elisha staged his encounter with Naaman to leave no doubt as to who was responsible for the miraculous healing that took place. By refusing to meet Naaman face-to-face, Elisha made him realize that healing came from God, not from the superstitious incantations of a human prophet (see 2 Kings 5:11). By demanding that Naaman wash in the Jordan River—instead of allowing him to wash in waters belonging to Aram and to Aram's gods—Elisha asserted the supremacy of Israel's God over Aramean idols.

The carefully orchestrated episode left its mark on Naaman, who declared afterward, "Now I know that there is no God in all the world except in Israel" (2 Kings 5:15). The irony of the story is that a pagan warrior's eyes were opened to what so few in Israel were able to see.

INSIGHT: Jesus mentioned Naaman as proof that ethnic or religious heritage does not entitle someone to God's favor. He noted that none of Israel's own lepers were healed in Elisha's time, but only Naaman (see Luke 4:24–27). Later Jesus commanded His followers to take the gospel to all nations, proving once more that God's love knows no geopolitical boundaries.

# NABAL

## Wealthy Fool Who Rebuffed David

And there was a man in Maon whose business was in Carmel.
The man was very rich; he had three thousand sheep and
a thousand goats. He was shearing his sheep in Carmel.
1 SAMUEL 25:2 ESV

Some people just seem to be begging for harm to come to them—the guy who flies down the highway at ninety miles per hour, the kids who play outside during a thunderstorm, the woman who shoplifts a few things here and there. Nabal, whose name appropriately means "fool," would have found good company with these people.

Nabal was a wealthy landowner who lived in Carmel, about fifteen miles west of En-gedi on the Dead Sea, the area where David and his men were hiding from Saul. David's men had been careful not to harass Nabal's servants as they looked after his huge flocks of sheep and goats, and David's men even provided protection for Nabal's flocks against bandits in the area (1 Samuel 25:15–16). So when the time came for Nabal to shear his sheep and reap the profits, David sent his men to ask for a gratuity. Nabal, true to his name, refused—and it was only the shrewd intervention of his wife that kept David from completely wiping out Nabal and his men. In the end, Nabal was struck dead by the Lord (1 Samuel 25:37–38), and David married his widow.

INFORMATION: David's wife Abigail, Nabal's widow, was later captured and carried off by Amalekites who raided the town of Ziklag while David was away. Ziklag had been given to David while he sought refuge from Saul in Philistia. When David learned about Abigail's capture, he quickly mobilized his men and pursued the Amalekites and destroyed them, recovering Abigail and the other captives. (Read the story in 1 Samuel 30.)

# NADAB
## First Son of Aaron

"Then bring near to you Aaron your brother, and his sons with him, from among the people of Israel, to serve me as priests—Aaron and Aaron's sons, Nadab and Abihu, Eleazar and Ithamar."
EXODUS 28:1 ESV

"It's not what you know, but who you know" can only get you so far. In the end, you will still be held responsible for your own actions.

As Aaron's firstborn son, Nadab witnessed the plagues in Egypt, saw God's people delivered through the Red Sea, and enjoyed the daily manna delivered to the Hebrew camp (Exodus 16). He tasted the waters of Marah and Elim (Exodus 15), saw water flow from a rock (Exodus 17), and probably saw for himself the tablets containing the Ten Commandments (Exodus 20). Being the son of Aaron and the nephew of Moses, Nadab certainly had a front-row seat from which to witness God's miraculous show of power.

Nadab also became one of Israel's first priests—a position that he qualified for because he descended from Aaron. He represented the people's sacrifices and concerns to God and helped care for the holy objects of worship. Because of his position, he was allowed to approach God on Mt. Sinai along with seventy elders of Israel (Exodus 24:1, 9).

But pedigree and position did not spare Nadab and his brother from God's judgment when they made an offering to God that did not meet His holy standards. Nadab and his brother were instantly killed, providing the people with a powerful reminder that God's holiness is not to be taken lightly by anyone.

INSIGHT: A commitment to Christian service can sometimes fizzle into complacency. While you might begin a ministry with the greatest of intentions, the constant repetitive tasks of the work may cause you to lose sight of its impact or holiness before God. Pray for a fresh and reverent perspective as you continue to serve in the ways God has appointed for you.

# NAOMI
## Mother-in-Law of Ruth

The women said to Naomi: "Praise be to the LORD, who this day has not left you without a guardian-redeemer. May he become famous throughout Israel!"

RUTH 4:14

Naomi needed a redeemer. Bereft of her husband and her sons, she had no one to care for her. At least that's how it seemed to her. Little did she know that God was already working to provide a redeemer.

Naomi was from Bethlehem in Judah, but a famine forced her and her family to move to the country of Moab on the other side of the Dead Sea. While there, Naomi's husband and two sons died. Eventually Naomi decided to return to Judah along with her Moabite daughter-in-law Ruth, who chose to leave her own family and people and follow Naomi and her God, the Lord.

When Naomi returned, she told her neighbors to stop calling her Naomi, which means "pleasant," and to call her Mara, which means "bitter," for she was suffering much. But God was already working to provide a redeemer for Naomi— a relative who would buy her property and marry Ruth to raise up a family with her in the name of her deceased husband.

Ruth began gleaning leftover grain from the fields of Naomi's distant relative Boaz, and Boaz took great interest in the younger woman. He lovingly provided for Ruth and Naomi and made sure Ruth was safe while she gleaned in his fields.

Eventually Boaz married Ruth and purchased the land of Naomi's, thereby ensuring that Ruth and Naomi would always be provided for. When Ruth bore a son to Boaz, the women of the town recognized the child as a redeemer who would help provide for Naomi (Ruth 1–4).

INSIGHT: According to the story, Naomi was blessed with not one but two redeemers—and the New Testament makes it clear that there is yet another Redeemer who always stands ready to help all who turn to Him: Jesus (Galatians 4:4–5; Titus 2:11–14).

# NEBUCHADNEZZAR
## King of Babylon

"Now I will give all your countries into the hands of my servant Nebuchadnezzar king of Babylon; I will make even the wild animals subject to him."
JEREMIAH 27:6

No pagan ruler played a more prominent role in the biblical drama than King Nebuchadnezzar of Babylon. Nebuchadnezzar's exploits are well documented in both scripture and extrabiblical sources.

After a successful career commanding the Babylonian army, Nebuchadnezzar inherited his father's throne near the end of the seventh century BC. He reigned more than four decades.

Among his many conquests, Nebuchadnezzar made numerous incursions into Jewish territory. Initially, Nebuchadnezzar allowed Judah's kings to remain on the throne, so long as they kept up their tribute payments. The first of these kings, Jehoiakim, rebelled, switching loyalties from Babylon to Egypt. In retaliation, Nebuchadnezzar removed Jehoiakim from the throne and plundered the temple. Jehoiakim's successors, Jehoiachin and Zedekiah, fared no better. Finally, in 586 BC, Nebuchadnezzar razed Jerusalem, destroyed the temple, and carried the surviving inhabitants into exile. The kingdom of Judah was defeated.

For all his pomp and power, though, Nebuchadnezzar was nothing more than God's instrument. The prophet Jeremiah revealed that it was God who gave Judah into Nebuchadnezzar's hands (see Jeremiah 21:7). God was responsible for his victories over Tyre and Egypt (see Ezekiel 29:17–20).

Once, in response to Daniel's successful interpretation of a dream, the Babylonian king had acknowledged the supremacy of Israel's God (see Daniel 2:46–47). Soon, however, Nebuchadnezzar forgot and attributed his successes to his own "mighty power" (Daniel 4:30). In response, God afflicted Nebuchadnezzar with temporary insanity—as He had promised earlier. Once his sanity was restored, Nebuchadnezzar acknowledged the supremacy of the Lord once more. "His dominion," Nebuchadnezzar declared, "is an eternal dominion" (Daniel 4:34).

INTERESTING. . . Nebuchadnezzar is a rare, pagan contributor to the Bible. The fourth chapter of Daniel is attributed to the Babylonian ruler. Nebuchadnezzar's adulation of the one true God seems to have represented something less than true conversion, as he alluded to Marduk (also known as Bel, for whom Daniel was renamed Belteshazzar) as "my god" (see Daniel 4:8).

# NEHEMIAH
## Persian Cupbearer and Jewish Reformer

Then I said to them, "You see the trouble we are in: Jerusalem lies in ruins, and its gates have been burned with fire. Come, let us rebuild the wall of Jerusalem, and we will no longer be in disgrace."
NEHEMIAH 2:17

Nehemiah had probably never set foot in his homeland when he took it upon himself to rebuild Jerusalem's wall. The city had been destroyed a century before his time.

But Nehemiah was ideally suited to the task—driven, determined, and unafraid to confront any obstacle. After all, this was a man who put his life on the line every day, serving as the Persian king's cupbearer.

As cupbearer, Nehemiah would taste the king's food and wine before giving it to him, making sure it had not been poisoned. Cupbearers enjoyed a revered status in the royal court, and Nehemiah took advantage of his close relationship with the king to make a bold request. Having been informed by his brother that Jerusalem was in a state of disrepair—despite the return of many exiles—Nehemiah requested a leave of absence to lead the rebuilding effort in his homeland. The king obliged, appointing Nehemiah as governor of Judah.

Upon his arrival in Jerusalem, Nehemiah set his sights on the city's most pressing need: a protective wall. Officials from Judah's neighboring provinces, including Sanballat, governor of Samaria, scoffed at the idea—first ridiculing Nehemiah's efforts, then plotting to undermine them by force. When these efforts failed, Sanballat accused Nehemiah of sedition. Such rivalry among Persian governors was not uncommon. In any case, Nehemiah persevered over the opposition from his enemies, completing the wall in less than two months.

INSIGHT: Nehemiah shared God's heart for the poor and His passion for justice. In order to pay the Persian king's tax, Jerusalem's poor had to borrow from the wealthy. But the wealthy smelled opportunity for enrichment and charged interest, forcing many to mortgage their own lands just to survive. In keeping with God's law (see Exodus 22:25–27), Nehemiah ended this practice, accusing the nobility of sending their own people into yet another form of exile: economic exploitation.

NEHEMIAH views the ruins of Jerusalem before beginning his work. Nothing in his life could have prepared him for the task—but he had faith to complete the work.

# NERO
## Deranged Roman Emperor

Let everyone be subject to the governing authorities, for there is no authority except that which God has established. The authorities that exist have been established by God.

ROMANS 13:1

Nero is not mentioned by name in the New Testament, but his impact on the fledgling church was so notorious that some early Christians came to regard him as the Antichrist.

Nero came to power in AD 54, aided by his scheming mother, Agrippina, who had charmed her way into the affections of Claudius, the previous emperor. Nero's mother very likely instigated Claudius's assassination by poisoning—and Nero seems to have inherited his mother's homicidal tendencies, arranging her own demise a few years later.

Nero was regarded as a megalomaniac. Much to the consternation of Rome's staid nobility, Nero loved to compose his own songs and perform them publicly. Desperate for adulation, Nero made an extended visit to Greece, where his flamboyant performances were more enthusiastically received. Just prior to his suicide, Nero is said to have lamented that the world was about to lose a great artist.

As emperor, Nero proved a menace to the church. When large sections of Rome burned to the ground in AD 64, Nero blamed the fire on the local Christian sect. According to the historian Tacitus, a contemporary of Nero, Rome's displaced population suspected its own emperor of arson. As an unpopular minority falsely accused of everything from orgies to cannibalism, Christians proved an easy scapegoat. On Nero's orders, a number of believers were brutally executed. Some were covered in animal skins and torn apart by dogs, others were crucified, and still others were lit as human torches.

This was the emperor to whom Paul appealed his case just a few years before the great fire (see Acts 25). As a Roman citizen, Paul had the right to personally defend himself before Caesar. While Paul's exact fate remains a matter of speculation, one early tradition held that Paul was beheaded on Nero's orders, shortly before the emperor's own downfall.

INSIGHT: Paul's teaching concerning the "governing authorities" (see Romans 13:1) is especially poignant when one considers just who the "governing authority" was at the time: Nero. Christians, Paul taught, are to be good citizens regardless of who sits on the throne.

To a man solely concerned with his own pleasure and power, Christians must have seemed laughably weak to NERO. But the faith remains long after the emperor and his empire passed away.

# NICODEMUS
## Religious Leader Taught by Jesus

"How can someone be born when they are old?" Nicodemus asked.
"Surely they cannot enter a second time into their mother's womb to be born!"
JOHN 3:4

Nicodemus's faith did not appear in a moment of sudden illumination. Rather, it seems to have emerged gradually.

The Bible captures just three episodes from Nicodemus's life—all of them recorded in the book of John. In the first scene, Nicodemus sought an audience with Jesus, hoping to hear more from the popular rabbi. The nighttime setting has led many to conclude that Nicodemus feared the consequences of being seen publicly with the controversial Jesus. In His encounter with Nicodemus, Jesus told the inquisitive Pharisee that no one could experience God's kingdom without being reborn. Nicodemus, unable to distinguish between "earthly things" and "heavenly things" (see John 3:12), received a mild rebuke, accompanied by further explanation. It was to Nicodemus that Jesus revealed that faith in God's Son leads to eternal life.

John does not indicate whether Nicodemus walked away from the conversation having put his faith in Jesus, but the other two episodes featuring the religious leader are revealing. As the conspiracy against Jesus developed, some of the religious leaders rebuked the temple guards for not arresting Jesus when they had the chance. In response, the guards came to Jesus' defense, to which the Pharisees retorted that since no religious leader had put his faith in Jesus, neither should the guards. Apparently contradicting this claim, Nicodemus spoke up, challenging his colleagues for condemning Jesus without a hearing.

Once more, however, Nicodemus disappeared from the scene as quickly as he had appeared. He did not reemerge until the death of Jesus, when he, along with Joseph of Arimathea, took Jesus' body from the cross and buried it in an unused tomb—one final tribute to the Messiah who had once shared with him the secret of eternal life.

INSIGHT: The phrase Jesus used to describe spiritual rebirth to Nicodemus can be translated "born again" or "born from above" (see John 3:3, 7). Either way, it describes a phenomenon that human beings are incapable of bringing about by their own will—we are wholly dependent on the grace of God.

When it was time to take the body of Jesus down off the cross, it was NICODEMUS—the Jewish leader who had once met with Jesus at night—who stepped up to assist Joseph of Arimathea with the anointing and burial.

Just like his ancestor Adam, NOAH was given the task of looking after God's creatures—and becoming a father to humanity.

# NOAH
## Builder of the Ark

By faith Noah, when warned about things not yet seen,
in holy fear built an ark to save his family.

HEBREWS 11:7

The unknown writer of Hebrews described Noah as a precursor of the kind of faith it would take to follow Christ. Noah's story was also a foreshadowing of the kind of redemption that God would provide for His people.

Noah lived during a time of rapidly escalating depravity. During this time, according to the author of Genesis, "every inclination" of the human heart had turned evil—much to God's anguish (see Genesis 6:5–6). As a "righteous man," Noah stood in marked contrast from the rest of civilization. Noah's righteousness was not superficial, yet it consisted of just one thing: Noah "walked with God" (see Genesis 6:9) while the rest of humanity walked in the other direction.

In Genesis, two descriptions of humanity's wickedness bookend the account of Noah's righteousness, evoking the impression that God's lone worshipper was in danger of drowning amid a sea of wickedness. God, however, had other plans—intending to drown humanity's wickedness in a sea of judgment, sparing only Noah and his family.

The details concerning Noah, the ark he built, and the flood that ensued are well-known. Acting on nothing but faith, Noah built the ark to God's exact specifications. Twice the writer noted that Noah did "all" or "everything" just as God commanded (see Genesis 6:22; 7:5).

As for the ark that Noah built, the Hebrew word is unique, used in Noah's story and in just one other place: the tale of the baby Moses being placed in a basket so he could escape Pharaoh's infanticide (see Exodus 2:3). Noah and his ark—and the deliverance it represented for those who follow God—anticipated the story of Moses and Israel's miraculous deliverance from the Egyptians. Also, according to the author of Hebrews, Noah's faith provided a model that all believers should follow in their devotion to Christ.

INTERESTING. . . There are other accounts of a catastrophic flood—complete with a Noah-like hero—besides the one found in the Bible. Other examples can be found in ancient Sumerian and Akkadian literature. In the Sumerian story, the hero is named Ziusuddu. In the famous *Epic of Gilgamesh*, the flood hero is named Utanapishtim.

# OBADIAH
## Prophet against Edom

"You should not gloat over your brother in the day of his misfortune,
nor rejoice over the people of Judah in the day of their destruction,
nor boast so much in the day of their trouble."
OBADIAH 12

Obadiah's tiny prophecy (his is the shortest book in the Bible) takes just moments to read. But for the nation of Edom—to whom it was directed—his words had a reverberating impact.

Aside from the meaning of his name, "servant of the Lord," nothing is known about Obadiah—neither his family, nor his home, nor his background is revealed in scripture. Obadiah's prophecy concerned the Edomites, longtime enemies of Israel. Centuries earlier, the Edomites had denied the Hebrews passage on their way to the Promised Land. King David eventually subjugated Edom, but the latter managed to wrest itself free from Jewish control.

The tension between Israel and Edom can be traced all the way back to their ancestors, Jacob and Esau. The two brothers were estranged when Jacob stole Esau's birthright. The Bible later reveals that God had chosen Jacob over Esau as heir to the Abrahamic covenant.

At the time of Obadiah's writing, Israel's and Edom's fortunes had been reversed. The people of Judah faced destruction, while the Edomites looked on and celebrated Judah's misfortune. Scholars have long debated whether Obadiah wrote about Jerusalem's destruction in 586 BC or some prior calamity—though the description in Obadiah 1:10–12 seems to indicate the former.

In any case, Obadiah admonished these distant cousins of the Israelites not to gloat over Judah's hardships, warning that the same fate awaited Edom. Obadiah envisioned a brighter future for the exiles of Israel, while Edom would be erased from history.

INSIGHT: The last words of Obadiah introduce what is perhaps the book's most important lesson: "The kingdom will be the Lord's," the prophet declared (Obadiah 21). At the end of all things, it is God—and no human power—that rules over the nations and the territories they possess.

# OG

## Amorite King

Then [the Israelites] turned and went up along the road toward Bashan, and Og king of Bashan and his whole army marched out to meet them in battle at Edrei.

NUMBERS 21:33

It's been said that the bigger they are, the harder they fall. Og certainly proved this cliché true.

Og controlled sixty cities—each of them boasting high walls and other defenses—in the territory of Bashan, which abutted the northeast corner of the Promised Land. As one of the obstacles the Israelites had to overcome before entering Canaan, Og's kingdom represented an imposing barrier to their inheritance of the land—and not just because of Bashan's well-fortified cities.

In his farewell speech to the Israelites, Moses remembered Og as the last of the Rephaites, an ancient race first mentioned in Genesis 14 when Abraham had to rescue his nephew Lot. The Rephaites were considered giants—as tall as the Anakites, according to Moses. (Years earlier, when Moses had commissioned several spies to report on the Promised Land, they had quailed at the sight of Anakites dwelling there.) As if to bring the point home, Moses reminded his audience of the size of Og's legendary iron bed: nine cubits—that is, thirteen feet long.

Og would have made a fierce enemy for Israel, except for one thing: God had promised to deliver him into Moses' hands—and not just Og, but his entire army and all sixty fortified cities. When Og and his army marched out to confront the Israelites—who had once lost their courage at the mere thought of combating giants—the battle was swift and decisive. The book of Numbers simply says, "So they struck him down, together with his sons and his whole army, leaving them no survivors" (Numbers 21:35). Og's defeat helped clear the Israelites' way into the Promised Land.

INTERESTING. . . Giants—unusually tall warriors—appear during a number of pivotal moments in Israel's story. In addition to the Anakites (who were crucial to Israel's unwillingness to enter the Promised Land at the first opportunity) and the Rephaites (among whom was Og), David famously felled the Philistine giant Goliath, winning the young warrior the favor of his fellow Israelites.

# OMRI
## King of Israel

But Omri did evil in the eyes of the LORD and sinned more than all those before him. He followed completely the ways of Jeroboam son of Nebat, committing the same sin Jeroboam had caused Israel to commit, so that they aroused the anger of the LORD, the God of Israel, by their worthless idols.
1 KINGS 16:25-26

Perhaps more is known about Omri from outside scripture than from the Bible itself. In fact, Omri is regarded as the most politically and militarily important monarch to sit on the throne of the northern kingdom of Israel. That, however, was not enough to salvage his reputation in the eyes of God.

With Omri's rise to power, Israel enjoyed a time of relative stability after a brief but intense period of volatility. Omri's dynasty endured for almost five decades—no small accomplishment by Israelite standards.

Omri's predecessor, Zimri, reigned for a mere seven days. Having murdered the previous king, Zimri declared himself ruler of Israel. At the time, Omri was leading the Israelite army in a siege against a Philistine stronghold. The military rejected Zimri's appointment as king, preferring their commander instead. So Omri marched on Israel's capital, which he took easily. Before he could be killed by Omri, Zimri committed suicide, setting his palace on fire. After besting yet another contender for power, Omri secured his place on the throne, which he occupied for twelve years.

As king, Omri made a number of strategic moves. Most importantly, he built the city of Samaria on a hill and made it his base of operations. The new Israelite capital was a much more defensible site than the one Omri had subdued. From the Bible we know that Omri lost territory to neighboring Syria (see 1 Kings 20:34), but extrabiblical sources reveal that he pressed his advantage against Moab, taking some of their lands. It is likely that Omri orchestrated a political arrangement with the Phoenicians, which led to his son Ahab's marriage to Jezebel.

For all his diplomatic and military success, the Bible judged Omri a failure. Not only did he persist in the idolatry of Israel's kings, but also the writer of 1 Kings concluded that Omri was even more sinful than any of his predecessors.

INSIGHT: It may seem surprising that the Bible did not include more details of Omri's reign, particularly since his tenure was reasonably well documented in extrabiblical sources. Omri's story is a useful reminder that God does not value success as the world defines it—what truly shapes a person's legacy is his or her faithfulness to the Lord.

# ONESIPHORUS
## Paul's Loyal Friend

May the Lord show mercy to the household of Onesiphorus,
because he often refreshed me and was not ashamed of his chains.

2 TIMOTHY 1:16

Some of the last recorded words of the apostle Paul contain a greeting to the household of Onesiphorus, the faithful friend who sought him out in Rome.

Onesiphorus is mentioned only in Paul's second letter to his disciple Timothy, pastor of the church in Ephesus. It was to be Paul's final letter, written sometime around AD 66 or 67. Rome had burned in a great fire just a few years before, and its deranged emperor, Nero, blamed the Christians in order to avoid Rome's suspicious glare at himself. As a result, believers in Rome were subjected to horrific persecution. Some were torn apart by wild animals, while others were burned alive. Paul, who had appealed his case to Caesar sometime before the great fire of Rome, was now imprisoned, in all likelihood nearing the end of his life. He had never felt more isolated—the apostle confided in Timothy that "everyone in the province of Asia [present-day western Turkey] has deserted me" (2 Timothy 1:15).

It was no small injury. Paul had invested much of his ministry—indeed much of himself—into that part of the world. Ephesus had been his home for more than two years. He had spent more time there than in any other city to which his missionary journeys had taken him. Paul had made disciples there, lectured in the public hall, cast out demons, and cured illnesses. Yet now, all that seemed forgotten—more to the point, he seemed forgotten as he languished in a Roman prison.

But Onesiphorus had not forgotten Paul. He made the eight-hundred-mile journey from Ephesus to Rome and searched hard until he found the imprisoned apostle. Such a journey was not without risk; Nero's persecution of the church at Rome had yet to subside. But that would not deter Onesiphorus. He did not mind being associated with a condemned man in chains. Onesiphorus had been Paul's faithful friend in Ephesus—now he was his loyal companion in Rome. Having been comforted, Paul asked God's blessing on Onesiphorus.

INSIGHT: Onesiphorus lived up to his name, which means "bringing profit." While others sought to profit only themselves, Onesiphorus traveled far to bring profit to another.

# ONESIMUS
## A Runaway Slave Who Gained a New Master

I [Paul] appeal to you [Philemon] for my son Onesimus, who became my son while I was in chains. Formerly he was useless to you, but now he has become useful both to you and to me.

PHILEMON 10-11

As songwriter Bob Dylan put it, "You're gonna have to serve somebody." If Onesimus had lived in our day, he couldn't have agreed more.

Onesimus, a slave of a Colossian believer named Philemon, had run away from his master and somehow ended up meeting Paul. In an amazing display of the power of the gospel to change lives, Onesimus apparently became a believer and agreed to return to Philemon to face whatever consequences awaited him. At the same time, Paul sent a letter (now known as the New Testament book of Philemon) with him telling Philemon of how useful Onesimus, whose name means "useful," had become to him. In the letter, Paul urged Philemon to welcome Onesimus back as a brother rather than a slave. Paul even asked Philemon to charge to him any debt incurred by Onesimus, although Paul was quick to point out that Philemon owed his very self to Paul—most likely meaning that Paul had led Philemon to Christ.

And just in case Philemon needed some extra encouragement, Paul asked him to prepare a guest room in case he happened to stop as he passed through Colosse! Surely the thought of physically looking Paul in the eye was all the motivation he needed to do the right thing.

INSIGHT: The question remains: Who are you going to serve? If you had asked Onesimus before he became a believer, he may have bitterly answered, "Philemon," or perhaps after he fled, "No one but myself." But in the end, we all serve somebody else—either the Lord or the devil. After Onesimus became a believer, he went back to Philemon perhaps expecting to return to a life of servitude, but really he was serving the Lord. Who are you going to serve?

A Roman slave serves wine in a mosaic from the second century, not many years after Paul's intercession for a slave named ONESIMUS.

# OTHNIEL
## Judge of Israel

So the land had peace for forty years, until Othniel son of Kenaz died.
JUDGES 3:11

As the first listed among a series of judges, Othniel's story established a pattern that would be repeated often in Israel's history.

Othniel had already proven his valor during the conquest of the Promised Land. He led the successful assault on Kiriath Sepher (in what became the territory of Judah) in order to win a girl's hand in marriage. (One detail that modern readers may find disturbing is that the girl in question was, in fact, his cousin.)

However, Israel failed to complete its conquest of the Promised Land. As a result, the pagan practices of the land's original inhabitants continued unabated. Soon the Israelites were copying their neighbors, forsaking God in order to worship Baal, the supreme Canaanite god, and Asherah, the Canaanite mother goddess, instead. As punishment, God sent raiders from Aram Naharaim (northern Mesopotamia, located in present-day Iraq) to oppress the Israelites. The punishment lasted eight years, until the Israelites remembered the real God and cried out for deliverance. In response, God raised up Othniel—one of the heroes of Canaan's conquest—to do the job.

As judge of Israel, Othniel fulfilled two functions: He served as a military commander in times of conflict and as political leader in times of peace. Othniel performed both tasks admirably. Without going into detail, the Bible simply says that Othniel overpowered the oppressors from Aram Naharaim (Judges 3:10). After that, the Israelites enjoyed a period of peace and prosperity that lasted until Othniel's death forty years later.

However, the writer did not leave Othniel's story before revealing the secret to his success as both ruler and warrior: Othniel had been filled with the "Spirit of the Lord" (Judges 3:10), empowered by God for the task at hand.

INTERESTING. . . Othniel had heroism in his blood. His uncle was Caleb, one of only two spies (the other being Joshua) who had encouraged the Israelites to enter the Promised Land as God had commanded.

# PASHUR
## Priest during Jeremiah's Time

> When the priest Pashhur son of Immer, the official in charge of the temple of the LORD, heard Jeremiah prophesying these things, he had Jeremiah the prophet beaten and put in the stocks.
>
> JEREMIAH 20:1-2

Pashhur appears only briefly in the Bible, but he played the antagonist in a bitter conflict with one of Israel's most polarizing prophets.

In the years leading up to Judah's exile, the priesthood had been compromised, becoming little more than a crutch to prop up a corrupt, wayward nation. God's blessing came to be taken for granted—as long as the temple stood and priests offered the designated sacrifices, what real harm could come to God's chosen nation?

Because the people forgot that God's blessing depended on their faithfulness, the stage was set for the confrontation between prophet and priest. Jeremiah (himself a member of the priestly class) railed against Judah's unfaithfulness. None—not even his fellow priests like Pashhur—were safe from the prophet's divinely inspired rage.

But Jeremiah did not just preach condemnation of sin—he foretold the demise of the entire nation, too. His words were regarded as unpatriotic, even treasonous. Jeremiah's prophecies threatened to send the entire nation into a panic (see Jeremiah 26:8–9). Because of this, Pashhur used his influence as the second highest-ranking priest in the temple to intimidate Jeremiah into silence. He ordered the prophet beaten and put in restraints for a day.

Apparently, Jeremiah failed to get the message. Pashhur, however, wound up with a new identity. After being released, Jeremiah declared that from now on, God's name for Pashhur was Magor-Missabib—Hebrew for "terror on every side." Not for the last time, Jeremiah predicted the downfall of his own country at the hands of Babylon.

INSIGHT: The incident involving Jeremiah and Pashhur contains a sobering lesson. Sometimes being faithful to God means we must do the unpopular, refusing to tow the party line or say what others want to hear. Jeremiah chose the path of unpopularity at great personal cost. Pashhur, on the other hand, chose not to listen and paid dearly for his error.

# PAUL
## Apostle to the Gentiles

*I have become all things to all people so that by all possible means I might save some. I do all this for the sake of the gospel, that I may share in its blessings.*
1 CORINTHIANS 9:22-23

The apostle Paul, the New Testament figure second only to Jesus in prominence, was a man of single-minded devotion. His mission to bring the gospel to the Gentile world filled him with an unrelenting fervor that carried him across the Roman Empire. In retrospect, Paul's background made him the perfect choice for this God-ordained mission.

Paul was born in the city of Tarsus (located in present-day Turkey), which was cosmopolitan and diverse; it was one of the leading university cities of its day. There Paul would have encountered all kinds of religious, cultural, and philosophical expressions.

But Paul was also devoted to the faith of his ancestors. He studied under Gamaliel, grandson of Hillel, the most famous rabbi of his day. As an adult, Paul bore all the markings of a rabbi. He even counted himself among the Pharisees.

Given his background, perhaps it is no surprise that God chose Paul to "proclaim my name to the Gentiles and their kings" (Acts 9:15). With one foot in the Jewish world and the other in the culture of the Gentiles, Paul was ideally suited to take the gospel from one to the other. His status as a Roman citizen—which suggests he belonged to the aristocracy—gave him enormous freedom as he traveled the empire. Paul used his citizenship not for his own gain, but to gain an audience with Caesar—knowing full well that to appeal to the Roman emperor (as only a Roman citizen could) was to put his very life at risk (see Acts 25:11). Paul's fate is not known. However, it is believed he gained his audience before Caesar—the dangerous Emperor Nero, to be precise—where he may well have become a martyr for the faith.

INSIGHT: Despite his justifiably revered status in church history, Paul comes across as a refreshingly human figure. He was passionate—capable of great fits of emotion. The book of Acts even records Paul's falling out with his colleague Barnabas (Acts 15:36–41). Paul knew that he was just a sinner—in his mind, "the worst of sinners" (1 Timothy 1:16)—who had been saved by God's immeasurable grace.

Saul of Tarsus—soon to be known as the apostle PAUL—falls from his horse upon seeing the Lord. The encounter would change his life.

Earthly powers put PETER in chains. Heavenly power put his guards to sleep, loosened the manacles, and opened the door of his jail.

# PETER
## Apostle of Jesus

But Peter declared, "Even if I have to die with you, I will never disown you."
And all the other disciples said the same.
MATTHEW 26:35

Peter is one of the most passionate, impetuous, and volatile characters in the Bible. As such, he was simultaneously capable of great triumph and enormous failure. Peter's boundless enthusiasm was exceeded only by his love for his Master, Jesus.

Peter's original name was Simon. However, Jesus liked to call him Cephas, an Aramaic word meaning "rock" or "stone," which translated into Greek as "Peter." During the course of Jesus' ministry, Peter emerged as the natural leader among the disciples. However, standing a head above the other disciples simply meant that Peter had further to fall—and he did. Immediately after his famous confession—which Jesus revealed was a result of divine enlightenment (see Matthew 16:17)—Peter proved equally adept at getting things wrong, contradicting Jesus' prediction of His own death (Matthew 16:22). Later, Peter confidently swore that he would stand with Jesus to the bitter end—that he would die with Jesus, if the need arose. Not for the first time, though, Peter had misunderstood the fundamental nature of Jesus' ministry. When guards came to arrest Jesus, Peter reached for his sword and attacked the servant of the high priest. Peter believed the time had come to fight, not realizing that Jesus' mission was to lay down His life. Most famously, Peter wound up disowning his Master three times, much to his own dismay.

Despite all of this, Jesus never gave up on Peter. According to Mark's Gospel, the angel at the tomb mentioned Peter by name when he told the women to share the news of Jesus' resurrection. Also, John recorded a particularly touching post-resurrection scene in which Jesus restored Peter, entrusting to him the vital task of shepherding the early church.

INTERESTING. . . . According to tradition, Peter was crucified for his faith. Some interpreters read Jesus' statement in John 21:18 ("When you are old you will stretch out your hands, and someone else will dress you and lead you where you do not want to go") as a prediction of his martyrdom. Legend has it that Peter requested to be crucified upside down because he did not consider himself worthy of being killed in the same manner as Jesus.

In their time, the PHARAOH was seen as a descendant of the sun god Ra. The Bible shows that he was no more than an instrument in the hands of the one true God.

# PHARAOH
## King with a Hard Heart

But when Pharaoh saw that there was a respite, he hardened his heart
and would not listen to them, as the LORD had said.

EXODUS 8:15 ESV

Pharaoh's determination to maintain power caused him to discount the obvious
hand of God. Although the Bible doesn't record the name of this Pharaoh (many
scholars think it may have been Menephtah, son of Ramses II), it does tell of his
ill-fated resolve.

As king of Egypt, Pharaoh struggled to maintain the power and order of
the land. The vast Hebrew population provided a significant labor source and
played an important role in Egypt's economy. As slaves, they helped build the
infrastructure of the land—creating construction supplies and buildings (Exodus
5). If Pharaoh had yielded to Moses' demands, it would have dealt a blow to the
kingdom, the economy, and his personal prestige.

Through Moses and Aaron, God inflicted Egypt with ten plagues designed
to induce Pharaoh to release the Hebrew people and send them on their way to
the Promised Land (Exodus 7–12). While many of the plagues initially motivated
Pharaoh to release God's people, he changed his mind and held on to the people as
soon as God removed the pain of the plague from the land. These plagues included
turning the water into blood, infestations of frogs, lice, flies, and the death of cattle.
They also included the infliction of boils, hail, locusts, and darkness.

Despite his grasping for power and his efforts to hold his kingdom's economy together, Pharaoh finally relented when the plagues became personal. The
tenth plague (the killing of the firstborn son) directly affected Pharaoh's life and
succession plan. Seeing his own dead son finally persuaded the king to release the
people.

INSIGHT: Pharaoh's stubbornness is no different than that of many
in the world today. When they read of supernatural events in the Bible
or hear of answered prayer, they explain away God's hand and continue
to ignore the reality of God. Be careful that you don't dismiss your
own blessings as good fortune or the mere fruits of your own hard
work. Thank God for the times He answers your prayers.

PHARISEES, at right, challenge Jesus over His disciples' snacking on grain they picked on the Sabbath day. Jesus' response? "The Sabbath was made for man, not man for the Sabbath," He told them. "So the Son of Man is Lord even of the Sabbath" (Mark 2:27–28).

# PHARISEES
## Jewish Religious Leaders

*"For I tell you that unless your righteousness surpasses
that of the Pharisees and the teachers of the law,
you will certainly not enter the kingdom of heaven."*
MATTHEW 5:20

Pharisees are a notorious and sometimes misunderstood group in the New Testament. While they provided one of the chief sources of opposition to Jesus, they actually had more in common with Him than some other Jewish religious groups of the day.

Some may be surprised to learn that Jesus shared two of the Pharisees' most important theological commitments. Unlike their rival Sadducees, Pharisees firmly believed in the bodily resurrection—a fact the apostle Paul later used to his advantage when he appeared before the Sanhedrin, a ruling body comprised of both Pharisees and Sadducees. On the basis of their shared belief in the resurrection, the Pharisees sided with Paul.

Jesus and the Pharisees also shared a deep devotion to the Torah, the Jewish law contained in the first five books of the Old Testament. The Pharisees were mainly preoccupied with how to interpret and apply the law, while Jesus insisted that He came not to abolish but to fulfill (that is, to give the ultimate interpretation or meaning to) the law (see Matthew 5:17).

Nevertheless, the New Testament records a profound rift between Jesus and the Pharisees. Out of their zeal for correct interpretation of the law, they had turned it into a burden. Often, their efforts to keep the letter of the law caused them to miss the *spirit* of the law, such as when they carefully tithed the smallest spices while neglecting matters of justice, mercy, and faithfulness (see Matthew 23:23–24). As lay leaders, the Pharisees were held in high esteem among the people—something they relished (see Luke 11:43). Because of this, it is no surprise that they vigorously opposed anyone who represented a threat to their power and influence. As the ultimate fulfillment of the law, Jesus represented precisely such a threat.

INTERESTING. . . The Pharisees were not necessarily united in their opposition to Jesus. The Gospel of John mentions one Pharisee, Nicodemus, who sought a personal meeting with Jesus and even defended Him (briefly) to his fellow Pharisees.

PHILIPPE G
1516.

TE S
OBIS

PHILIP's enthusiasm for evangelism was such that he ran to share the gospel with the Ethiopian eunuch.

# PHILIP
## Evangelist

Philip went down to a city in Samaria and proclaimed the Messiah there.
When the crowds heard Philip and saw the signs he performed,
they all paid close attention to what he said.
ACTS 8:5-6

In His great commission to the disciples, Jesus revealed that His gospel was to smash all ethnic, national, and cultural barriers. Philip the evangelist embraced the inclusive nature of the gospel with inspiring zeal.

Philip was first mentioned as one of seven men chosen by the apostles to care for the widows who belonged to the Jerusalem church. Even this seemingly small service was a barrier-breaking act—Philip and his colleagues were responsible for making sure that the widows were treated equally, regardless of whether they were Hellenistic (Greek) or Hebraic Jews.

Later, when Saul's persecution scattered the church of Jerusalem, Philip seized the opportunity to go to Samaria. By extending the good news of Jesus, the Jewish Messiah, to the Samaritans, Philip shattered another centuries-old barrier.

The great evangelist was not finished with his barrier-breaking career, either. Having been directed by an angel, Philip journeyed from Jerusalem to Gaza, meeting an Ethiopian eunuch along the way. This man had two strikes against him. First, he was not Jewish (not even part Jewish, as the Samaritans were). Second, as a eunuch, Jewish law regarded him as ritually unclean—he was, in effect, "damaged goods." Yet Philip did not hesitate to sit with the eunuch and explain the gospel to him. The real test, however, came when the eunuch asked to be baptized. By agreeing to perform the ancient purification ritual, Philip acknowledged that in God's eyes, the eunuch was clean, pure, and whole.

Philip's life became the first of many signs that the good news of Jesus is for all people.

INTERESTING. . . The name Philip means "one who loves horses" in Greek. In the case of Philip the evangelist, this turned out to be an appropriate name, since he had to run up to a horse-drawn chariot in order to engage the Ethiopian eunuch in conversation! (See Acts 8.)

# PHILISTINES
## Enemies of Israel

Wail, you gate! Howl, you city! Melt away, all you Philistines! A cloud of smoke comes from the north, and there is not a straggler in its ranks.
ISAIAH 14:31

From the time of the judges and lasting for the duration of the monarchy, the Philistines were a thorn in Israel's side. They had settled in the Promised Land long before God's chosen people arrived; but like the Israelites, they started out as immigrants from a distant land.

The Philistines—from which we get the word *Palestine*—were also known as the Sea Peoples. It is believed they originated from the Aegean Sea region, which comprises mainland Greece, Turkey, and the islands in between. Being accustomed to the sea, the Philistines settled the coastal region of the Promised Land, from the border with Egypt in the south to Gaza in the north.

On their way into the Promised Land, the Israelites took the longer route in order to avoid "Philistine country" (Exodus 13:17). In an allusion to what was to come, the writer of Exodus noted that the Israelites were not yet prepared for war.

Eventually war was what they got. Having failed to subdue the Philistines during the conquest, the Israelites often found themselves oppressed by the Philistines during the time of the judges. The Philistine threat was undoubtedly a factor in Israel's desire for a king. After three centuries of conflict, the Israelites wanted a strong leader to fight for them (see 1 Samuel 8:20). Their first choice, Saul, proved largely ineffective—he was, in fact, eventually killed in battle with the Philistines. However, Saul's successor, King David, managed to subdue the Philistines during his reign.

INTERESTING. . . Before he was king, David lived under the protection of Achish, the Philistine ruler of Gath. David was very nearly pressed into service to fight against his fellow Israelites, but at the last minute, Achish changed his mind on the advice of his military commanders, who did not trust David (see 1 Samuel 28:1–2, 29).

# PHINEHAS
## Son of Eli

Eli's sons were scoundrels; they had no regard for the LORD.
1 SAMUEL 2:12

Phinehas made a mockery of the priesthood. In the end, though, he paid dearly for his sin.

Phinehas was the younger son of Eli, a priest in the sanctuary at Shiloh before the temple was built in Jerusalem. While Eli was a reasonably honorable man—albeit an overindulgent father—the text had no kind words for his sons, Hophni and Phinehas. The two served alongside their father, but according to scripture, they were "scoundrels"—literally, "sons of worthlessness" (1 Samuel 2:12).

Phinehas's utter disregard for God was demonstrated by his abuse of the fellowship offering. The law made provision for a sacrifice to celebrate the peace between God and His people—this was the fellowship offering. It was unique in that all parties involved received a portion of the sacrifice. The first and best portion (including the fat and internal organs) belonged to God, while the priest and those making the sacrifice shared the remaining meat. According to tradition, the priest would plunge an instrument into the meat while it cooked. Whatever came out—however large or small—was his portion.

But Phinehas demanded his portion first, before the meat had been cooked. In doing so, he cheated both God (by claiming the best part for himself) and the person offering the sacrifice (presumably by taking more than his rightful share). Worse, if anyone challenged Phinehas's behavior, he was threatened with violence.

As if this weren't bad enough, Phinehas and his brother engaged in sexual immorality with women who served near the sanctuary entrance. It came as little surprise when God struck down Phinehas and his brother as they carried the ark of the covenant into battle against the Philistines.

INSIGHT: Eli and the rest of Israel paid dearly for Phinehas's sin. Stunned by the news of his son's death, Eli fell backward and died. Phinehas's widow named their son Ichabod, meaning "the glory has departed from Israel," accurately capturing the despair her people felt over the loss of the ark in battle. Often the consequences of our sin reach far beyond our own lives.

POTIPHAR's wife appears much more often in art than Potiphar himself—but in this seventeenth-century painting by the Dutch master Rembrandt, Potiphar listens to his wife's accusation against Joseph.

# POTIPHAR
## Owner of Joseph

Meanwhile, the Midianites sold Joseph in Egypt to Potiphar, one of Pharaoh's officials, the captain of the guard.

GENESIS 37:36

Potiphar was very fortunate to be master of a slave whose every move was blessed by God. Unfortunately, Potiphar's good fortune was not destined to last.

Potiphar was an important individual—a high-ranking official in Pharaoh's court. His obvious wealth is confirmed by the fact that he was able to afford a slave in the first place. After a few weeks with Joseph, however, Potiphar must have been thinking that he had gotten quite a bargain.

Potiphar quickly recognized the divine blessing on Joseph, and soon the latter was more than a common slave; he was Potiphar's personal attendant. Thanks to Joseph, Potiphar did not have a care in the world—at least as far as his household was concerned—for he had Joseph to look after everything for him. Joseph managed everything at home and in Potiphar's fields. All Potiphar had left to worry about was what to eat for dinner.

Unfortunately for Potiphar, he should have been a bit more worried about his wife, who eventually became attracted to his talented, young attendant. Joseph, however, clung to his integrity and resisted each of her advances. Frustrated and rejected, Potiphar's wife sought revenge, falsely accusing Joseph of attempted rape. Potiphar fell for the ruse, believing himself a fool to have trusted Joseph so completely. He had Joseph put into the royal prison; it was the second time Joseph found himself bound against his will.

However, God's blessing did not end when Joseph was taken from Potiphar's household. Joseph continued his rise to prominence, while Potiphar and his devious wife faded into obscurity.

INTERESTING. . . Potiphar is part of an interesting pattern in Joseph's story. Three times Joseph found favor in the eyes of a superior—first as the favorite of his own father, then with Potiphar, and finally with Pharaoh himself. Each time, Joseph encountered some kind of trial—first being sold into slavery, then being imprisoned, and finally coming face-to-face with the brothers who betrayed him—only to triumph in the end.

# QUEEN OF SHEBA
Solomon's Royal Visitor

Arriving at Jerusalem with a very great caravan—with camels carrying spices, large quantities of gold, and precious stones—she came to Solomon and talked with him about all that she had on her mind.

1 KINGS 10:2

According to the writer of 1 Kings, the queen of Sheba visited Solomon in order to test him. The queen's test may well have demanded the best of not only Solomon's wisdom but his diplomatic and political skills as well.

The Bible does not reveal origins or the identity of the queen of Sheba. According to one tradition, she came from Ethiopia. (Ancient Ethiopian lore claimed that Solomon and the queen had a son who grew up to become the African nation's first king.) However, archaeological findings indicate that the Arabian Peninsula is a more likely option. It is also a location that fits well with the biblical narrative.

The ancient peoples of Arabia had accumulated great wealth by importing goods from Asia and Africa and exporting them to their neighbors in the Middle East. Their trade consisted mainly of expensive spices, gold, and precious stones—in other words, the very items the queen presented to Solomon.

Under Solomon, Israel had become a regional power—his kingdom controlled some of the key trade routes that Sheba depended on for its prosperity. In all likelihood, this is what the queen of Sheba "had on her mind" when she tested Solomon's wisdom. Between Solomon's impressive showing—his skills at discernment and negotiation were legendary (see 1 Kings 3:16–28)—and the overwhelming display of his wealth, the queen was awestruck. She honored Israel's king with high praise and a lavish gift of gold, about four-and-a-half tons' worth. Solomon reciprocated by giving the queen "all she desired" (1 Kings 10:13). The queen of Sheba returned to Arabia, her diplomatic mission a success.

INSIGHT: Jesus taught that the queen of Sheba (to whom he referred as the "Queen of the South" in Matthew 12:42 and Luke 11:31) was more righteous than the religious leaders who opposed Him. When they skeptically demanded proof of His authority, Jesus responded that the queen herself would judge people like them. After all, at least she—though she was a foreigner—had been willing to listen to Solomon's wisdom. Jesus' words are a reminder that religious piety has no value unless it is accompanied by a humble, teachable heart.

The QUEEN OF SHEBA was a great power in her own right, but she acknowledged and respected Solomon's God-given wisdom.

# RAHAB
## Righteous Prostitute

By faith Rahab the prostitute did not perish with those who were disobedient, because she had given a friendly welcome to the spies.
HEBREWS 11:31 ESV

You rarely hear the word *righteous* used to describe a prostitute, but that's how the Bible depicts Rahab (James 2:25). Though God did not condone her occupation, Rahab's faith in God and her protective actions of the Hebrew spies made her righteous in God's eyes.

When the Hebrew people were finally ready to take possession of the Promised Land, Joshua sent two spies into Jericho to size up the enemy (Joshua 2). The spies found safe refuge in the home of a prostitute, where it would not have been unusual for people to be seen coming and going. With such potential activity, the men found her residence a practical place to hide and spend the night. While at her home, the spies were buoyed by the city residents' fear of the Hebrews and by the help extended to them by Rahab.

In exchange for her protection, the spies gave Rahab instructions that would keep her and her family safe during the upcoming battle. By following these directives, her life was spared when the city was ravaged. As her final reward, she received an honored place in Israel's history; for in addition to New Testament references that laud her faith, some Jewish traditions indicate that Rahab became the wife of Joshua, the Hebrew leader.

INFORMATION: The story of Rahab goes beyond the pages of Joshua and continues into the New Testament Gospels. Tucked in the genealogy of Jesus, we find an unlikely ancestor of the long-awaited Messiah: Rahab. By including unlikely women like Rahab (the prostitute) and Tamar (the woman who had a child with her own father-in-law), God revealed that the Messiah would be the Savior of all people—the likable *and* the undesirables (Matthew 1:5).

God certainly works in mysterious ways: The Hebrew spies could hardly have expected help from such an unlikely source as RAHAB, and a woman disrespected by almost everyone because of her occupation could hardly have expected to be rewarded by God.

# REUBEN
## Son of Jacob

The sons of Reuben the firstborn of Israel (he was the firstborn, but when he defiled his father's marriage bed, his rights as firstborn were given to the sons of Joseph son of Israel; so he could not be listed in the genealogical record in accordance with his birthright).

1 CHRONICLES 5:1

Reuben's life was a tragic tale of honor lost and never quite regained. Reuben forfeited the double portion of the inheritance that should have been his by right as the firstborn of Jacob by his first wife, Leah. More important, Reuben was forced to relinquish his prized position as the leader among the twelve tribes of Israel.

After Rachel died while giving birth to Jacob's youngest son, Benjamin, the family moved south to Migdal Eder. There Reuben did the unthinkable: He slept with his father's concubine, Bilhah.

Bilhah had been Rachel's servant. Years earlier Rachel had offered her to Jacob to be his concubine, in the hopes that Bilhah would bear the children that Rachel was unable to conceive. By sleeping with Bilhah after Rachel's death, Reuben did more than commit an act of sexual immorality—he signaled his rejection of Jacob's authority as family patriarch. In the ancient world, one way to challenge a king's rule was to sleep with one or more of his concubines. Such an insult—usually committed by another family member—communicated one's own claim to the throne and invariably severed ties with the king. Reuben, perhaps sensing his father's weakness, overstepped his bounds as firstborn and presumed to supplant his father as head of the family.

The other episodes from Reuben's life reveal a more honorable character. When his brothers conspired to murder Joseph, it was Reuben who intervened, persuading them to throw Joseph in a cistern instead. Before Reuben could rescue Joseph as he had planned, his brothers sold the boy to a passing caravan of Midianite merchants.

INTERESTING. . . Jacob never forgot his son's betrayal. While commending him for his honor and strength, the aging patriarch told Reuben that he would no longer excel. The blessing of preeminence passed to Judah, while Joseph's sons inherited the rights of the firstborn.

# REZIN
## King of Aram

> Then Rezin king of Aram and Pekah son of Remaliah
> king of Israel marched up to fight against Jerusalem
> and besieged Ahaz, but they could not overpower him.
>
> 2 KINGS 16:5

Solomon wisely wrote, "If a man digs a pit, he will fall into it; if a man rolls a stone, it will roll back on him" (Proverbs 26:27). This could not have been truer of King Rezin of Aram.

Rezin ruled over Aram, a nation to the northeast of Israel and Judah that occasionally fought with them over territory. It seems that Rezin was trying to form an alliance of nations to resist the advance of the growing Assyrian Empire, but when King Ahaz of Judah refused to join, Rezin teamed up with King Pekah of Israel, and perhaps even with the Edomites and the Philistines, to attack Judah (2 Kings 16; 2 Chronicles 28:16–19).

In an act of desperation, Ahaz turned to Assyria to help him. He made Judah a subservient kingdom to Assyria and paid the king of Assyria a large amount of silver and gold to attack Rezin and Pekah. The plan worked. The Assyrians annexed the territory of Aram and much of Israel, and they killed Rezin. Unfortunately, this also appears to have whetted the Assyrians' appetite for the region, because they later returned and attacked Judah as well.

INFORMATION: Isaiah prophesied about Rezin's downfall to Assyria in Isaiah 7–9. He called Rezin and Pekah "two smoldering stubs of firewood" (Isaiah 7:4) and assured Ahaz that they would not succeed. Sadly, Ahaz did not trust the Lord and took matters into his own hands to gain the help of Assyria.

RUTH gleans grain as the field's owner, Boaz, watches from a distance. In time, the two will be married.

# RUTH
## Moabite Daughter-in-Law of Naomi

But Ruth replied [to Naomi], "Don't urge me to leave you or to turn back from you. Where you go I will go, and where you stay I will stay. Your people will be my people and your God my God. Where you die I will die, and there I will be buried."

RUTH 1:16-17

Going the extra mile for someone can be difficult, even when life is going well. But when there is adversity and personal turmoil, making an extra effort to help someone else can seem impossible. In the character of Ruth, however, we see a shining example of someone doing the impossible.

During the time of the judges in Israel, the family of Elimelek and Naomi moved to Moab to escape a famine in Judah. While they were there, one of their sons married a Moabite woman named Ruth. After ten years of marriage and the earlier death of her father-in-law, Ruth's husband also died.

Naomi, also widowed, decided to return to Judah with her husbandless daughters-in-law. On the way, Naomi told them both to return to their mothers' homes, while she continued on alone to Judah. One daughter-in-law agreed, but Ruth adamantly refused to leave Naomi. She stayed with her and helped to provide food for herself and Naomi in Judah by gleaning in nearby fields—where she eventually met and married Boaz, the landowner, a relative of Elimelek. Boaz and Ruth later had a son, Obed, who became the grandfather of King David.

INSIGHT: Even though Ruth may have been suffering tremendous grief over the death of her husband, she didn't return home to the possible comfort of her own family and people. She went with Naomi to a strange land with strange customs, providing comfort and help to her mother-in-law. In our own times of personal distress, would we show others this same selfless kindness? We can rely on God to provide for all our emotional and physical needs—so that we can then demonstrate His love and care to others.

# SADDUCEES
## Jewish Religious Leaders

The Sadducees say that there is no resurrection, and that there are neither angels nor spirits, but the Pharisees believe all these things.
ACTS 23:8

The Sadducees were one of two groups—the other being the Pharisees—that famously came into conflict with Jesus. Of the two, however, Sadducees did not have as much direct contact with Jesus, perhaps because their values and ideals were even further removed from Jesus than were those of the Pharisees.

Unlike the Pharisees, who found favor with the common people of Palestine, the Sadducees were "men of the world." They moved comfortably along the halls of power, rubbing shoulders with the religious and political elite. Whereas the Pharisees stood out for their strict adherence to the Law, Sadducees had a talent for blending in—they were happy to accommodate their Roman overlords in order to maintain their own grasp on power. Many Sadducees were thought to be members of the priestly class. As a political party, the Sadducees held sway over the Sanhedrin, the Jewish ruling council.

In terms of their theology, Sadducees were, once again, men of the world. According to the New Testament, they did not believe in the immortality of the soul or the existence of angels or spirits. According to them, this life is all there is—and they sought to make the most of it.

Without doubt, the more prominence Jesus gained, the more of a threat He became to the Sadducees' comfortable arrangement with Rome.

INTERESTING. . . Paul brilliantly used the polarizing subject of the resurrection to send the Sanhedrin into an uproar when he was made to appear before them. When he claimed that he was on trial because of his belief in the resurrection, he angered the Sadducees who were present, while gaining the sympathy of their rival Pharisees (see Acts 23:1–11).

# SAMARITAN WOMAN
## Woman Who Met Jesus at a Well

Then, leaving her water jar, the woman went back to the town
and said to the people, "Come, see a man who told me
everything I ever did. Could this be the Christ?"

JOHN 4:28-29

The Samaritan woman must have hated coming to fetch water day after day from the well—all that work, all that gossip about her and her shameful marital situation—but it was at that very well that she found the source of living water, which truly satisfies and brings eternal life.

The Samaritans lived in the north-central part of Israel, and they were descended from both Jews and foreign peoples who had been relocated to Israel by the Assyrians hundreds of years earlier. Jews and Samaritans typically despised each other.

When Jesus was traveling from Jerusalem to Galilee, He took the most direct route and passed through Samaria where He met a woman at a well at midday. Jesus spoke to her and offered her living water that brings eternal life, rather than merely water from the well that needed to be fetched day after day. Jesus revealed to the woman that He was aware of her many marital relationships and her current situation of living with a man who was not her husband, and taught her about true worship. She was amazed and went back to her town to tell everyone about Jesus. Many Samaritans turned to Jesus because of the woman's testimony (John 4).

INTERESTING. . . In the language of Jesus' day, the word for "living" water is the same for "running" water—like a river. The Samaritan was initially interested in Jesus' offer of "living/running" water to avoid having to come to the well each day. Jesus, however, gave her something that truly satisfies the soul.

SAMSON was famously a powerful man, but his victory over the lion made it plain that he drew his strength from the spirit of God.

# SAMSON

## Judge and Strongman of Israel

"You will become pregnant and have a son whose head is never to be touched by a razor because the boy is to be a Nazirite, dedicated to God from the womb. He will take the lead in delivering Israel from the hands of the Philistines."

JUDGES 13:5

People have married for a host of unusual reasons, but Samson is perhaps one of the few in history to have wedded for the express purpose of picking a fight with the bride's extended family.

Samson was born to Manoah and his wife—a righteous couple who had been barren for years. God revealed that just as Samson's birth was special, so, too, was his life to be special. He was to be set apart, bound by a lifelong Nazirite vow. In the Bible, people were set apart not just for the sake of being different—such honor always had a specific purpose. Samson's purpose was to begin the rebellion against Israel's most notorious oppressors, the Philistines.

As required by the rules governing Nazirite vows, Samson was expected to abstain from three things: alcohol, contact with anything unclean (such as dead bodies), and haircuts.

Before he died, Samson probably violated all three requirements. He behaved as if he were above any rule or responsibility. Even his choice of a wife was baffling to his God-fearing parents, for Samson had demanded to be united to a Philistine woman. This, however, turned out to be one of God's strategic masterstrokes—the writer of 1 Samuel revealed that God used this marriage as an opportunity for Samson to confront the Philistines.

Samson did just that. After Samson decimated their crops, the Philistines murdered Samson's wife and father-in-law. Samson retaliated by going on a violent rampage, nearly bringing the Philistines and their Israelite subjects to full-scale war. In the end, another woman named Delilah proved to be Samson's undoing, and Samson's greatest achievement—the destruction of the temple to Dagon and the slaughter of everyone in it—brought about his own death, too.

INSIGHT: Even though the book of Judges portrayed his life as something of a profitable disaster, Samson still managed to earn a mention—albeit a passing one—in the "faith hall of fame" found in the book of Hebrews. Samson's life is an object lesson of both the high cost of sin and God's ability to bring victory from even our greatest failures.

# SAUL
## Israel's First King

"To obey is better than sacrifice, and to heed is better than the fat of rams. . . .
Because you have rejected the word of the LORD, he has rejected you as king."
1 SAMUEL 15:22–23

As far as disasters go, Saul's time on the throne was an unmitigated one. At first, the man with the impressive physique tried to resist his appointment as king of Israel. He did not consider himself suited to the job. He was, as he reminded Samuel, a member of "the smallest tribe of Israel"; his clan was "the least of all the clans of the tribe of Benjamin" (1 Samuel 9:21). Apparently, many of Saul's own subjects were inclined to agree. After his first coronation, some openly questioned whether Saul was up to the job of delivering Israel.

Soon, however, Saul won over the doubters when he rallied a massive army to come to the aid of Jabesh Gilead, just east of the Jordan River. The victory prompted a second coronation ceremony—this one marked by the people's enthusiastic celebration of their new king.

Unfortunately, Saul's triumph was short-lived. For the rest of his reign, he proved erratic and unstable. More than once he failed to listen to the prophet Samuel—as a result, Samuel announced that the throne would be taken from Saul. When God chose David as Saul's successor, the king of Israel became even more dangerously paranoid. Though David would not lift a finger against him, Saul made repeated attempts on the young warrior's life. So obsessed was Saul that he slaughtered eighty-five priests suspected of aiding David and even began neglecting his royal duties. While Saul schemed, it was left to David to deliver the town of Keilah from the Philistines—the very enemy whom Saul had been raised up to fight.

Saul's life ended in humiliating defeat to the Philistines. His failure was complete, and the nation of Israel was in disarray.

INSIGHT: Despite being enemies, David never completely lost his regard for Saul. Such was David's honor that on the first occasion when he spared Saul's life, he was "conscience-stricken" over merely cutting a corner of his robe (see 1 Samuel 24:5). When Saul was finally killed, David responded with a touching lament for Israel's fallen king (2 Samuel 1:19–27). Long before Jesus came, David demonstrated what it looks like to "love your enemies" (see Matthew 5:44).

Elie Marcuse depicts the last moments of King SAUL's life in dark tones reflecting the state of Saul's heart at this point: a once good and humble man brought down by self-reliance, fear, and distance from the Lord.

# SENNACHERIB
## King of Assyria

So the LORD saved Hezekiah and the people of Jerusalem from the hand
of Sennacherib king of Assyria and from the hand of all others.
He took care of them on every side.
2 CHRONICLES 32:22

There are wicked people in this world who wield great power, and it can seem at times as if they are on the verge of completely overwhelming God's people. But we must always remember that God is infinitely more powerful than any human being—even someone so powerful as King Sennacherib of Assyria, the greatest power the world had ever known.

Up to the reign of Sennacherib, the Assyrian Empire appeared to be unstoppable. It was gobbling up virtually the entire civilized world of the Near East, and it had annexed the northern kingdom of Israel into its territory as well. After King Hezekiah of Judah refused to submit to Assyria and pay the tribute owed, King Sennacherib came and attacked the towns of Judah. Nearly all the fortified towns of Judah had fallen to Assyria—except for the capital city of Jerusalem. The Assyrians were besieging the city, and Hezekiah and his people were desperately crying out to the Lord to save them (2 Kings 18:13–19:34).

The Lord answered their prayers by sending an angel throughout the Assyrian camp—killing 185,000 troops in a single night! As a result, Sennacherib broke camp and returned to Nineveh, where his own sons killed him (2 Kings 19:35–37). Such is the amazing power of God.

INFORMATION: Among the ruins of Assyria's palaces in Nineveh, archaeologists have found wall reliefs depicting the siege of Lachish, one the towns of Judah captured by Sennacherib.

# SHAMGAR
## Judge of Israel

"In the days of Shamgar son of Anath, in the days of Jael,
the highways were abandoned; travelers took to winding paths."
JUDGES 5:6

Shamgar is perhaps the most unusual deliverer—and his account the shortest—
featured in the book of Judges.

According to the author, Shamgar followed Ehud, who sneaked a sword into
the palace of Eglon, king of Moab, and killed him. Following the assassination of
Moab's king, Ehud led the Israelites in battle, where they killed around ten thousand Moabite soldiers. And though the Moabite threat was neutralized, the writer
introduced a new danger: the Philistines who lived along the coast. They would
prove to be one of Israel's most persistent and dangerous enemies. To deal with
them, God raised up a man named Shamgar.

What makes Shamgar so unusual is his name—it is not a Hebrew name.
Nor was his hometown, Beth Anath, a Hebrew town. Located in the territory
of Naphtali, Beth Anath was a Canaanite town that was subjugated but not destroyed by the Israelites. The residents of Beth Anath had been allowed to live as
forced laborers. While the text yields no further clues about Shamgar's identity,
the strong implication is that he was foreign—in all likelihood a Canaanite.

The text does not bother to clarify whether Shamgar acted specifically in
Israel's defense or simply out of a mutual hatred for the Philistines. In any case,
Shamgar used an oxgoad—a wooden device with a sharp metal tip—to great ef-
fect, slaying six hundred Philistines. Almost as if anticipating Hebrew skepticism
at the thought of a Canaanite deliverer, the writer simply states, "He too saved
Israel" (Judges 3:31).

INSIGHT: Shamgar is yet another reminder of God's prerogative to
use anyone—even the unlikeliest of people—to achieve His sovereign
plan. God's purposes have always transcended nationality and ethnicity
(see Genesis 12:3).

# SHEM
## Noah's Son

[Noah] also said, "Praise be to the LORD, the God of Shem!
May Canaan be the slave of Shem."
GENESIS 9:26

Going into the ark prior to the great Flood, Shem had no children. After the waters receded, though, Shem became the ancestor of many great nations—including the chosen people of Israel.

Shem was the oldest son of Noah, the most righteous man on earth at the time. (Not that there was much competition.) Shem and his brother, Japheth—the youngest of Noah's three sons—seemed to follow in their father's footsteps, unlike the middle child, Ham.

The writer of Genesis recorded just one incident from Shem's life, but it was enough to reveal his character. After the Flood, Noah returned to his original livelihood: farming. Specifically, Noah decided to plant a vineyard. It is possible that Noah was the first person to do so—which would make Noah the world's original winemaker. Noah, however, enjoyed a little too much of his own harvest and became drunk on the wine he had made. Intoxicated, Noah retired to his tent, where he lay naked and unconscious. Ham walked in on his exposed father and seemed to find the situation amusing.

Ever since Adam and Eve's fall from grace in the Garden of Eden, nakedness had become synonymous with shame. Instead of doing the honorable thing and covering his father's nakedness—and thereby his shame—Ham told Shem and Japheth about it, apparently thinking they would find the situation as entertaining as he did. Shem, however, showed his father the respect he deserved; he and Japheth discreetly covered Noah, taking care to walk backwards into the tent so as not to see their father's nakedness.

It may seem like a silly episode, but the real issue was one of honor. Ham failed to demonstrate even the most basic respect for his father. Shem, on the other hand, did the right thing—and his descendants were rewarded for his honorable behavior.

INTERESTING. . . Shem is regarded as the ancestor of Semitic people groups, including the Jews. According to Luke, Jesus descended from Shem's third son, Arphaxad (see Luke 3:36).

SHEM wrestles a piece of wood while neighborhood men help construct the ark behind him. Only Shem and seven other family members will survive the coming worldwide flood.

# THE SHEPHERDS OF THE CHRISTMAS STORY
## Jesus' First Visitors

When the angels had left them and gone into heaven, the shepherds said to one another, "Let's go to Bethlehem and see this thing that has happened, which the Lord has told us about."
LUKE 2:15

If a child was born into a royal family today, there would be no end to the list of dignitaries who would be expected to visit the family and congratulate them. But when Jesus, the King of kings was born, the only people who even received an announcement were some lowly shepherds who might be compared to field hands today.

Because of the nature of their work, shepherds were often seen as dirty, low-class, uncivilized people in Bible times. Their full-time job, night and day, was to look after their flocks of sheep or goats, leading them to pasture and water and away from danger. At times they even acted as the doorway to their sheep pens by sleeping across the opening. Kings were often regarded as shepherds over their people, but a king's life actually had little in common with the rustic, austere life of those who looked after flocks of animals.

But it was to such people—and only to such people—that the angels announced Jesus' birth. The angels appeared to them and told them where they could find the child—and the shepherds responded in faith and went. After they visited Jesus and His family, the shepherds returned to their fields, praising God for all that they had seen and telling everyone they met about it, too (Luke 2).

INSIGHT: Thankfully, God's measure of human worth has little in common with our measure. We tend to value appearance, prestige, wealth, or power, but God does not seem to be swayed by any of these things. God regarded the presence of some lowly shepherds as fitting honor for the birth of His only Son, the King of kings.

THE SHEPHERDS OF THE CHRISTMAS STORY kneel at the manger holding the baby Jesus. The stained glass window is from a church in Stockholm, Sweden.

# SILAS
## Leader of the Early Church

About midnight Paul and Silas were praying and singing hymns to God, and the other prisoners were listening to them. Suddenly there was such a violent earthquake that the foundations of the prison were shaken.
ACTS 16:25-26

Silas was a gifted leader and a fearless adventurer. In addition, he may have aided in the composition of at least one New Testament book.

As a leader in the Jerusalem church, Silas was among those chosen to deliver the congregation's letter to Gentile believers in Antioch, Syria, and Cilicia. Silas lent credibility to the expedition, which also included Paul, Barnabas, and Judas Barsabbas. Silas, however, was far more than a letter carrier—in Antioch, he further encouraged the believers by prophesying to them. The content of Silas's teaching is not revealed in the book of Acts, but the result was that all the Gentile Christians were greatly encouraged.

Later, when Paul and Barnabas parted ways over their disagreement concerning Mark (see Acts 15:36–41), Paul invited Silas to accompany him to Syria and Cilicia. Their plans changed abruptly, however, when Paul received a vision of a man begging them to come to Macedonia. With that, the pair introduced the Gospel to present-day Greece. They were even imprisoned during their stay in Philippi. After a massive earthquake, however, their jailer (who was amazed to discover that Silas and Paul had not seized their opportunity to flee) converted to Christianity and invited them to his house. After that, the two were released.

Silas made an ideal traveling companion for Paul. Both were Roman citizens (see Acts 16:37), a fact that proved useful for getting out of difficult situations like the one at Philippi. Silas may have also had a way with words. Both letters to the church at Thessalonica were said to be from "Paul, Silas, and Timothy" (see 1 Thessalonians 1:1; 2 Thessalonians 1:1). Years later, the apostle Peter credited Silas with helping him write his first letter (see 1 Peter 5:12). Although he did not play a leading role himself, Silas proved a vital partner to two of the early church's greatest apostles.

INTERESTING. . . In three New Testament books (2 Corinthians, 1 Thessalonians, and 1 Peter) Silas is referred to as "Silvanus." Apparently "Silas" was a contraction of his full name.

# SIMEON
## Son of Jacob

"Simeon and Levi are brothers—their swords are weapons of violence. . . .
Cursed be their anger, so fierce, and their fury, so cruel!"
GENESIS 49:5, 7

Simeon was the second son born to Jacob by his wife Leah. Though she was convinced that her son's birth would win Jacob's affection, in the end her son Simeon revealed a violent streak that endangered the entire family.

When his sister, Dinah, was raped by a neighboring Hivite named Shechem, Simeon was furious. Perhaps just as outrageous to him as the original offense was the fact that his father, Jacob, did nothing in response. The writer of Genesis seemed sympathetic to Simeon and his brothers' reaction, calling Shechem's crime an "outrageous thing. . .that should not be done" (Genesis 34:7). However, Jacob's reaction was understandable, too. Yes, his daughter had been violated—but if he struck against his more powerful neighbors, he might put the whole family in jeopardy.

That, however, was not enough to pacify Simeon. It is no wonder that he and Levi led their brothers in their quest for revenge. They—along with Reuben, Judah, Issachar, and Zebulun—were Dinah's full brothers. So when Shechem brazenly asked for Dinah's hand in marriage, the brothers devised a cunning scheme. They demanded Shechem and his fellow Hivites circumcise themselves. Three days later, while they were still writhing in pain, Simeon and Levi led the slaughter. Simeon's only other significant contribution to the story in Genesis was as a hostage in Egypt. When Joseph sent his brothers home to fetch Benjamin, Simeon was detained, kept back as collateral to ensure the brothers' return.

After that, Simeon faded into obscurity—literally. Just as his father, Jacob, predicted on his deathbed, Simeon's descendants were scattered, their allotment in the Promised Land being surrounded on all sides by Judah.

INTERESTING. . . The sons of Simeon had at least one fleeting moment of glory. In the waning days of the southern kingdom—during the rule of Hezekiah—the Simeonites waged assaults against a number of Israel's enemies, including the dreaded Amalekites (see 1 Chronicles 4:41–43). After the exile, however, the tribe of Simeon was never again mentioned by name (except briefly in Revelation 7:7).

SIMON's sorcery had "amazed all the people of Samaria" (Acts 8:9)—but his "great power" was nothing compared to the power of God through Peter.

# SIMON
## The Sorcerer

> When Simon saw that the Spirit was given at the laying on of the apostles' hands, he offered them money and said, "Give me also this ability so that everyone on whom I lay my hands may receive the Holy Spirit."
>
> ACTS 8:18-19

Before the gospel came to Samaria, Simon was a minor phenomenon with a major ego. Pretending to be someone important—perhaps even claiming to be the incarnation of God Himself (depending on the meaning of the phrase "Great Power" in Acts 8:10)—Simon wowed the people with his sorcery, convincing them that he exercised control over the spiritual realm. In a time when most people assumed the existence of a spiritual world—and believed that it was not likely a benevolent force—sorcerers like Simon were in great demand.

But all that was before the arrival of Philip, the man famous for taking the gospel to unexpected places. As a follower of the resurrected Jesus, Philip possessed a power that made Simon look like the conjurer of cheap tricks by comparison. Even Simon was impressed—so much so that he "believed and was baptized" (Acts 8:13).

However, Simon seems to have been drawn to the power rather than to its source. When Peter and John came to impart the Holy Spirit to the Samaritan believers, Simon was beside himself. Desperate for his former glory, he offered the apostles money in exchange for the ability to dispense God's Spirit. After all, he had spent years pretending to do just that; now, he thought, the real thing was within his grasp!

How wrong he was. Enraged, Peter reduced Simon to a whimpering wreck, denying him any part in their ministry and warning him to beg God's forgiveness before it was too late. Nothing more is said about Simon, except that he begged Peter to pray on his behalf—now afraid to even speak to the God whose power he just tried to purchase.

INSIGHT: Simon had a fundamentally flawed understanding of the Holy Spirit. While Peter and John freely shared the Spirit, empowering all who believed, Simon saw the Holy Spirit as a means of gaining power for himself—some deep magic that he could dispense for a price. Peter and John did not use their status to control others but to release them from sin so they could experience Christ's promise of true liberation.

SOLOMON shows his amazing, God-given wisdom by deciding who was the real mother of a disputed baby. By ordering the child cut in half and divided between the women, Solomon knew the real mother would immediately give up her argument to protect the child. When she did, he awarded the baby to her.

# SOLOMON
## King of Israel

> "So give your servant a discerning heart to govern your
> people and to distinguish between right and wrong.
> For who is able to govern this great people of yours?"
> 1 KINGS 3:9

Solomon had everything going for him: wisdom, wealth, and power. Unfortunately, he had many vices as well: greed, lust, and idolatry. These combined to bring about the undoing of Israel in more ways than one.

Solomon was not the obvious choice for the throne. Nevertheless, David handpicked Solomon as his successor. While Solomon eventually took his place as one of the few truly great kings of Israel, he was very different from his father. David was a warrior, accustomed to dealing with conflict (or at least the threat of conflict) for most of his rule. By contrast, Solomon presided over the most enduring peace in Israel's history.

Without pressures from beyond his kingdom, Solomon devoted himself to other pursuits—namely, cultivating wisdom (which he famously displayed to the amazement of his subjects and foreign dignitaries alike), forging diplomatic alliances with regional powers like Egypt, and building the temple in Jerusalem.

Solomon, however, was not without his blind spots. His wisdom (a gift from God, according to the writer of 1 Kings) did not prevent him from plunging headlong into the dangerous pursuit of wealth. He accumulated chariots and horses in violation of God's command (see Deuteronomy 17:16). He used forced labor to build the temple and taxed the people heavily in order to finance his luxurious lifestyle (see 1 Kings 5:13; 12:4). Solomon's best-known weakness, however, was his taste for women—and lots of them. Solomon famously had seven hundred wives—many of them no doubt marriages arranged for diplomatic reasons—and another three hundred concubines. Like the practice of accumulating wealth, the king's taking of many wives was expressly forbidden by the Law (see Deuteronomy 17:17), and for good reason. Over time, Solomon's pagan wives lured him away from the one true God. And as the story ends, the once-wise king descends into folly.

INSIGHT: When he dedicated the temple, Solomon expressed a profound truth about God: No building can contain His presence (see 2 Chronicles 6:18–21). God in His grace condescends to move among us, but His presence and power cannot be confined to any building or box.

# TAMAR
## Daughter-in-Law of Judah

Judah recognized them and said, "She is more righteous than I, since I wouldn't give her to my son Shelah." And he did not sleep with her again.
GENESIS 38:26

As a two-time widow with no other real prospects, Tamar was in a no-win situation.

Tamar was the first wife of Er, Judah's oldest son. Judah had arranged the marriage himself—unfortunately, Er was guilty of some unspecified sin and died before producing an heir. As was the custom of the day, Judah then gave Onan, his second son, to Tamar. But history repeated itself. Onan died, too, leaving Tamar still without a son. Women who had no sons or husbands were vulnerable indeed. Judah had promised his third son to Tamar—just as soon as he was old enough to marry—but the years began to pass, and it became clear that Judah had no intention of keeping his word.

One day, after getting word that Judah was out and about, Tamar covered her face with a veil and situated herself on the road, waiting for Judah to pass. Pretending to be a prostitute, she solicited her own father-in-law, who just recently finished mourning his deceased wife. Not having anything with which to pay a prostitute, Judah gave Tamar his seal—sometimes attached to a cord and worn like a necklace—and staff as a pledge of good faith.

Three months later, when Tamar was no longer able to hide her pregnancy, Judah ordered her burned alive for her adultery. This was Tamar's no-win situation: As long as she was pledged to Judah's third son, she could not enter into another man's protection, but Judah had not kept his word and had failed to provide the protection Tamar needed. Judah had been a poor father-in-law, a fact that dawned on him when Tamar produced his seal and staff, saving her own life and the lives of her twin sons. Judah was shamed into acknowledging that Tamar was more righteous than he had been.

INSIGHT: While not condoning Tamar and Judah's sexual immorality in any way, the writer of Genesis seemed far more troubled about Judah's failure to meet his obligations to his family. Judah's story is an example of what can happen when God's people forget that the second greatest command in the whole Bible is to "love your neighbor as yourself" (see Matthew 22:37–39).

An obviously pregnant TAMAR, ordered burned to death for harlotry by her father-in-law Judah, produces the seal and staff of the man whose baby she carries: Judah.

The Bible never names THE THIEVES WHO WERE CRUCIFIED with Jesus—but some traditions give the name Dismas to the one who asked Jesus to "remember me when you come into your kingdom" (Luke 23:42).

# THE THIEVES WHO WERE CRUCIFIED

## They Died Alongside Jesus

> One of the criminals who hung there hurled insults at him:
> "Aren't you the Messiah? Save yourself and us!"
> LUKE 23:39

The precise identity of the men crucified alongside Jesus remains a mystery—as do their specific crimes. Though both died on their crosses, the two men experienced very different fates.

The three Gospels that mention the "thieves" (as tradition has come to identify them) refer to them in three different ways. According to Matthew, the two men were "robbers" or "rebels," depending on how the text is translated. Luke referred to them as "criminals," while Mark ambiguously described them as "those crucified with" Jesus.

Though it is not possible to state conclusively, it may be that the two men crucified next to Jesus were actual rebels, guilty of the crime (treason) for which Jesus was wrongfully condemned.

At first, both criminals were defiant and joined in the insults being hurled at Jesus. Who knows what motivated their vitriol—perhaps they did not think Jesus was "worthy" of being crucified alongside them. Or perhaps their agony simply revealed the worst of their characters. For whatever reason, though, one of the criminals had a change of heart, recorded only in Luke. Rebuking the other condemned man, he turned to Jesus and asked to be remembered in His kingdom—a powerful demonstration of his last-minute belief that not even death could keep God's kingdom from breaking into our world through the man who was dying next to him.

INTERESTING. . .Jesus' promise to the believing criminal (Luke 23:43) contains an interesting ambiguity. The meaning of the word *today* is reasonably straightforward, but what it refers to is less clear. It could be an indication that Jesus and the criminal would be together in paradise later that same day. Or Jesus simply may have been saying, in effect, "Today I'm telling you. . . ." The lack of punctuation in the oldest Greek manuscripts makes interpreting this nuance of the verse challenging.

"Doubting THOMAS" had said that he needed to see and touch Jesus' wounds before he would believe the Lord had returned from death. Here, in a painting by Rembrandt, Jesus shows Thomas the mark in His side left by a Roman soldier's spear.

# THOMAS
## Doubting Apostle

Then Jesus told him, "Because you have seen me, you have believed;
blessed are those who have not seen and yet have believed."

JOHN 20:29

Thomas is best known for his doubting tendencies, but the disciple of Jesus also known as Didymus was capable of demonstrating courage and resolve, too.

When his friend Lazarus died, Jesus set out for Bethany, near Jerusalem—not to pay His last respects, but to raise Lazarus from the dead. However, doing so meant walking straight into His enemies' lair. The disciples were aware of the dangers. Jesus had already alluded to His death (see John 10:15), and of course they were not blind to opposition of the religious leaders. They knew going to Bethany was risky. Yet Thomas alone spoke in favor of Jesus' plan, saying that if their Master was going to die, the rest of them may as well die with Him.

This episode of courage is overshadowed by Thomas's infamous display of doubt following the resurrection of Jesus. Thomas had been away when Jesus first appeared to the disciples. Upon hearing the news, he refused to believe it—until Jesus appeared yet again, astonishing the skeptical disciple.

It is easy to judge Thomas harshly. However, to do so is to forget that bodily resurrections were not exactly an everyday occurrence in the first century. Even the fact that Thomas had seen his Master raise others from the dead could have been forgotten easily in the grief and confusion that followed Jesus' crucifixion.

Thomas was not condemned by Jesus, nor was his belief rejected. Nevertheless, the risen Lord used the occasion to bless those who would believe in Him even without seeing.

INTERESTING. . . There are competing accounts of Thomas's life following the resurrection of Jesus. According to one tradition, he ventured as far as India. However, the early church theologian Origen wrote that Thomas brought the gospel to Parthia, which included parts of present-day Turkey, Iraq, and Iran. He is said to have died in Edessa, present-day Turkey. Whatever his contribution to the spread of Christianity may have been, Thomas was almost certainly a part of it. After all, he was present with the other disciples after Jesus ascended to heaven (see Acts 1:13).

# TIGLATH-PILESER
## King of Assyria

> Ahaz sent messengers to say to Tiglath-Pileser king of Assyria, "I am your servant and vassal. Come up and save me out of the hand of the king of Aram and of the king of Israel, who are attacking me."
> 2 KINGS 16:7

Never make a deal with the devil. Inevitably the price you pay is far greater than any benefit you receive, just as it was for King Ahaz of Judah when he appealed to King Tiglath-Pileser of Assyria for help against his enemy.

The mighty Assyrian Empire was on the rise during the reign of Tiglath-Pileser, but up to the time of Ahaz, they had not made any real forays into Israel. That all changed once Tiglath-Pileser got a taste of what lay in store in the area—thanks to Ahaz.

At some point in Ahaz's reign, the kings of Aram and Israel teamed up to attack Judah, and Ahaz—in a moment of desperation—appealed to Tiglath-Pileser for help. Ahaz voluntarily made Judah a subservient kingdom to Assyria and paid Tiglath-Pileser a large amount of silver and gold to attack Aram and Israel. Tiglath-Pileser agreed and attacked both Aram and Israel, as Ahaz had requested (2 Kings 16:1–9).

Unfortunately, however, Ahaz's actions piqued Assyria's interest in the region. Assyria would later capture all of Israel and attack Judah, as well.

---

INFORMATION: Isaiah prophesied about Tiglath-Pileser's attack on Aram and Israel in Isaiah 7–9. He assured Ahaz that a child would be born, and "before the boy knows enough to reject the wrong and choose the right, the land of the two kings you dread will be laid waste" (Isaiah 7:16).

# TITUS
## Paul's Ministry Partner

> But God, who comforts the downcast, comforted us by the coming of Titus, and not only by his coming but also by the comfort you had given him.
>
> 2 CORINTHIANS 7:6-7

On more than one occasion, Titus proved a vital partner in Paul's "ministry of reconciliation" (see 2 Corinthians 5:18).

In Paul's mind, Titus provided the answer to a burning question that motivated his letter to the Galatians: Was it necessary for Gentile converts to Christianity to be circumcised in order to be received into the body of Christ? According to Paul, Titus was living, breathing proof that the answer was no.

Titus is not mentioned by name in the book of Acts, though some have suggested (with good reason) that Titus was at the center of the circumcision debate described in Acts 15. In any case, Paul peppered his letters with numbers of references to Titus, demonstrating how important he was to Paul in their mutual ministry.

During his first missionary journey, Paul became the first church leader to systematically reach out to Gentiles wherever he went. At the close of this expedition, he returned to Jerusalem, presumably to join the debate over the need for Gentile circumcision (compare Galatians 2:1 with Acts 15:1, though some think Paul was referring to the visit alluded to in Acts 11:30). Some in the church at Jerusalem argued that circumcision was a necessary prerequisite for salvation. Before long, the same idea was circulating among believers in Galatia. Paul reminded his readers that not only had the church leaders in Jerusalem endorsed his ministry to the Gentiles, they had declined to make Titus—a Gentile believer who accompanied Paul to Jerusalem—undergo circumcision. In Paul's mind, Titus's example settled the matter.

In the years that followed, Titus continued to be a catalyst for reconciliation. Titus was Paul's emissary to the church in Corinth during a particularly difficult time in the relationship between it and the apostle. Much to Paul's relief, Titus returned to him with a positive report of comfort, "godly sorrow," and reconciliation (see 2 Corinthians 7:5-13).

Titus continued to work alongside Paul, traveling with him to Crete, where they seem to have parted for a time. Nevertheless, Titus continued to serve God faithfully, reconciling people to Him and to each other.

INTERESTING. . . Titus eventually wound up ministering in Dalmatia, a Roman province on the other side of the Adriatic Sea from Italy.

King UZZIAH, now a leprous outcast, in a seventeenth-century painting by the Dutch master Rembrandt.

# UZZIAH
## King of Judah

> But after Uzziah became powerful, his pride led to his downfall. He was unfaithful to the LORD his God, and entered the temple of the LORD to burn incense on the altar of incense.
>
> 2 CHRONICLES 26:16

Uzziah (known in 2 Kings as Azariah) was very nearly one of the great kings of Judah. Unfortunately, his pride and reckless ambition got in his way.

Uzziah's father, Amaziah, had died at the hands of his own people in the twenty-ninth year of his reign. But unlike Israel, where new (and often short-lived) dynasties routinely replaced one another, Judah had been promised an unbroken chain of kingly succession. So Amaziah's death did not bring the end of his dynasty. Instead, Uzziah—who had probably reigned as coregent for several years—was crowned king of Judah.

Uzziah got off to a good—albeit not great—start. He received a largely favorable assessment from the writers of both 2 Kings and 2 Chronicles, even though he failed to remove the "high places" where people offered their own sacrifices. On the military front, Uzziah was an unqualified success—perhaps the greatest warrior-king since David. With God's help, he subdued two of Judah's longstanding enemies, the Philistines and the Ammonites. He even extended Judah's territory, regaining access to the Red Sea via the Gulf of Aqaba. His country secure, Uzziah set about strengthening Jerusalem's defenses.

Unfortunately, Uzziah—who had once taken counsel from a godly teacher named Zechariah—let his success go to his head. He became proud and sought to inject his influence into the priestly arena. Uzziah paid dearly for his overreaching. God struck Uzziah with leprosy, a humiliating disease that rendered him ceremonially unclean—unable to fulfill his kingly duties or to set foot in the temple ever again.

INSIGHT: The English historian Lord Acton famously said, "Power tends to corrupt, and absolute power corrupts absolutely." Therein lays Uzziah's downfall—and perhaps the reason that God had separated the duties of priest and king in the first place. The Bible reveals that human beings cannot be trusted with too much power over others. As the writer of 2 Chronicles reminded his readers, Uzziah was a success "until he became powerful" and forgot the Lord (2 Chronicles 26:15).

THE WOMAN CAUGHT IN ADULTERY was undoubtedly a sinner—but her accusers unwittingly brought her to the one whose mission on earth was to save sinners and reconcile them with God.

# THE WOMAN CAUGHT IN ADULTERY
## Unnamed Woman Spared by Jesus

Jesus straightened up and asked her, "Woman, where are they? Has no one condemned you?" "No one, sir," she said. "Then neither do I condemn you," Jesus declared. "Go now and leave your life of sin."

JOHN 8:10-11

When the Jewish religious leaders dragged the adulterous woman before Jesus, He did not question her guilt. However, the entire situation reeked of injustice—which Jesus masterfully exposed in His response.

The adulterous woman provided the bait in the Pharisees' trap. Aside from this, nothing is known about her—or how the religious leaders managed to catch her "in the act" of committing adultery. They pretended to be concerned with fidelity to the Law of Moses, yet nothing could have been further from the truth. Otherwise, they would have apprehended the guilty man as well, since the Law held *both* parties accountable in cases of adultery (see Leviticus 20:10).

The religious leaders intended to use the woman's plight in order to trap Jesus in a no-win situation. If He disagreed with the suggestion that she be stoned, He would be accused of going against the Torah—the very Law He had come to "fulfill" (see Matthew 5:17). But if Jesus agreed with their sentence, He would be challenging the power of Rome, which had the exclusive authority to mete out capital punishment.

Perhaps the woman held her breath as Jesus invited the religious leaders to stone her—provided they were without sin themselves, that is. According to Jesus, only a righteous judge would do—and the only truly righteous judge in their midst (the Lord Himself) chose not to throw any stones. Instead, having silenced His opponents, Jesus sent the woman on her way, with the loving admonition to leave behind the destructive life that had gotten her into this mess in the first place.

INTERESTING. . . The earliest manuscripts of John do not contain this story of the woman caught in adultery. As further evidence that it was not original to John's Gospel, some experts note that the first verse (John 7:53) does not fit the preceding context. However, the story is consistent with the overall life and teachings of Jesus, leading a number of scholars to conclude that it is nonetheless authentic—just misplaced somehow. (There's even one family of manuscripts that puts the story at the end of Luke 21.)

# XERXES
## King of Persia

This is what happened during the time of Xerxes, the Xerxes who ruled over 127 provinces stretching from India to Cush.
ESTHER 1:1

Do you ever feel as if you are completely at the mercy of godless leaders? God's people in the days of King Xerxes must have felt the same. But, as the book of Esther shows, God's plans are never frustrated by sinful people—and He can even use those same people to accomplish His will.

Clearly Xerxes was a sinful unbeliever, and he ruled over the greatest empire of his day. Over a century earlier, the lands of Israel and Judah had been conquered and Jews were scattered throughout the Near East, ruled by Xerxes. Neither Xerxes nor most of his officials worshipped God, and a plot had even been hatched to exterminate all the Jews. Where was God? What was to become of His people?

Not to fear. God was still God, and Xerxes could do only what God allowed. The story of Esther describes how God orchestrated events so that Esther gained favor in Xerxes's eyes as one of his wives—and she was able to reveal the evil plot to him. In the end, God's people were saved, and Xerxes himself ordered the execution of those who had arranged for the Jews' destruction (Esther 9:14). Xerxes even promoted Esther's relative to the second-highest position in the empire!

INTERESTING. . . Xerxes is usually identified by scholars as King Xerxes I of Persia. This is the same Xerxes whose mighty army was delayed for three days at Thermopylae by three hundred Spartan warriors and whose fleet was destroyed by other Greek city-states at Salamis.

# ZADOK
## Priest during David's Time

But Zadok the priest, Benaiah son of Jehoiada, Nathan the prophet,
Shimei and Rei and David's special guard did not join Adonijah.

1 KINGS 1:8

Zadok, a direct descendant of Aaron, was one of David's most loyal allies, even in his darkest moments.

Aside from a passing reference in the context of David's consolidation of power (see 2 Samuel 8), Zadok first appeared in the story after David was unseated in a coup led by his own son Absalom. Zadok decided to accompany the king as he fled Jerusalem. More important, Zadok and his fellow priests meant to take the ark of the covenant with them—a powerful sign that in their estimation, David was still the rightful king and the recipient of God's blessing.

David wisely counseled Zadok to turn back. He knew from previous history that the ark was no magic token—but most of all, it was meant to stay in God's chosen city, among God's chosen people. Zadok obediently returned to Jerusalem, where he paved the way for David's triumphant return following Absalom's death.

Before David died, Zadok had one more opportunity to demonstrate his loyalty to Israel's greatest king. David's intent was for Solomon to succeed him as king. However, when Adonijah moved to preemptively install himself as David's successor, a number of David's advisers—including the priest Abiathar—rallied to him. Zadok, however, stood by the dying king's wishes. Together with the prophet Nathan, Zadok had the honor of anointing Israel's next rightful king, Solomon. Zadok ended up replacing Abiathar as well.

INTERESTING. . . Zadok's descendants served in the temple until the destruction of Jerusalem in 586 BC. According to the prophet Ezekiel, they alone were worthy to enter God's sanctuary, because they alone had remained pure while the rest of the Israelites strayed from God (see Ezekiel 44:15–16).

# ZECHARIAH
## Father of John the Baptist

Zechariah asked the angel, "How can I be sure of this?
I am an old man and my wife is well along in years."
LUKE 1:18

Though he may have had a rather common name (there are no less than twelve Zechariahs mentioned in the Bible), this particular Zechariah stood out as father to the forerunner of the Messiah.

Zechariah and his wife, Elizabeth, echoed a recurring theme from the Jewish story: barrenness and the accompanying sense of emptiness. In their world, bearing children meant the all-important survival of the family line. Being unable to conceive was taken as the absence of God's blessing.

However, Zechariah had been blessed in other ways, and there was no question of his integrity. A member of the Levite priestly class, he belonged to one of twenty-four divisions (his was the division of Abijah) that took turns serving in the temple at Jerusalem. According to the Gospel writer Luke, both he and his wife were blameless in God's sight. Luke wanted to make sure his readers understood that their barren situation was in no way the result of some undisclosed sin.

One day during his service, Zechariah was chosen to burn incense before the Most Holy Place inside the temple. Given the number of priests available for service, it was not an honor that one received very often. For Zechariah, an already unforgettable experience was made even more unusual by the appearance of an angel who announced the impossible: Zechariah and Elizabeth would bear a son. Their son would be subject to a lifetime Nazirite vow, much like Samson, and he would be counted as the greatest of the old prophets (see Matthew 11:7–13).

Zechariah seemed to believe it was too good to be true, despite knowing the stories of Sarah, Rebekah, Rachel, and Hannah. In response to his demand for a sign, the angel gave him one: He would be mute until the child was born. Having gotten the message but being unable to share it with others (see Luke 1:22), Zechariah returned home. Everything happened just as the angel said it would.

INTERESTING. . . Zechariah appeared once more in the story, overruling the custom of naming the firstborn after the father in order to obey the angel's instructions. The story reveals that the naming of the child, which took place at his circumcision on the eighth day, was apparently a community affair.

The elderly ZECHARIAH and his young son John (to be known as John the Baptist) meet with Mary and the young Jesus. The sixteenth-century painting is by the Italian artist Lorenzo Lotto.

# ZECHARIAH
## King of Israel

So the word of the LORD spoken to Jehu was fulfilled: "Your descendants will sit on the throne of Israel to the fourth generation."
2 KINGS 15:12

Zechariah's reign marked the beginning of the end for the northern kingdom of Israel—the final, tumultuous thirty years before the Assyrian Empire finally sacked Samaria. He was the exclamation point on the last period of relative calm ever seen in the northern kingdom.

Before Zechariah, Israel's monarchy had enjoyed four peaceful successions. Zechariah inherited the throne from his father, Jeroboam II, who inherited it from Zechariah's grandfather, Jehoash, who inherited it from Zechariah's great-grandfather, Jehoahaz, who inherited the throne from Zechariah's great-great-grandfather, Joash.

After Zechariah, only one of Israel's remaining kings successfully transferred power to his son. Only one died under peaceful conditions. Four, including Zechariah, were assassinated by their successors. One was carried off into exile in 722 BC, when the Assyrians descended on the land as instruments of God's judgment.

The four kings that preceded Zechariah averaged over thirty years apiece on the throne. His father, Jeroboam II, reigned for more than four decades. Together, Zechariah and the kings who followed him averaged less than seven years each. Zechariah himself only managed six months on the throne—a rather embarrassing performance, compared to the standard set by the rest of his family.

Like his royal predecessors, Zechariah did evil in God's sight—he perpetuated the sins of his fathers, worshipping false gods. By this time, though, God had had enough. The endgame had begun. Zechariah was assassinated in front of his own people. Instead of his son, Zechariah's assassin, Shallum, succeeded him as king.

INSIGHT: If Zechariah had paid more attention to God, perhaps the end would not have come as much of a shock. Years before, God had promised Zechariah's great-great-grandfather Joash that his dynasty would last four generations—God's reward to Joash (the closest thing Israel ever had to a good king) for purging the northern kingdom of Ahab's family and their idolatry. With the ascent of Zechariah, God's promise had been fulfilled—and with his death, the monarchy descended into chaos.

# ZECHARIAH
## Prophet

*This is what the Lord says: "I will return to Zion and dwell in Jerusalem. Then Jerusalem will be called the City of Truth, and the mountain of the LORD Almighty will be called the Holy Mountain."*

ZECHARIAH 8:3

For ten years, Jerusalem's most important construction site fell silent as work on the second temple ground to a halt. Zechariah was one of the prophets who stepped into the silence and summoned the people back to work.

Zechariah served a dual function in Jewish society: he was both prophet and priest. The grandson of Iddo had been born in exile. As such, he had not participated in the sin that brought God's wrath and led to the destruction of Jerusalem and its most precious building, the temple. Until his return to Jerusalem sometime in the 530s BC, Zechariah had been without a homeland. Even upon his return, he was still without a place to carry out his divinely appointed profession. Zechariah was a priest without a temple.

Work on the new temple began almost immediately after Cyrus, king of Persia, allowed the first delegation of exiles to return home. However, some of their neighbors objected to the new temple and managed to convince the royal authorities that the Israelites had a long history of rebellion and could not be trusted. As a result, work on the temple stopped for a full decade.

That all changed, however, when Zechariah began to prophesy, encouraging the people to resume work on the temple. According to the prophet, the completion of the temple would be a confirmation of God's presence. It did not matter that the new structure would not match the glory of Solomon's temple—the "day of small things" was not to be despised (see Zechariah 4:8–10).

Having been persuaded to return to work, the people of Jerusalem completed the temple in four years. Zechariah—who, according to Ezra, was instrumental in motivating the people to carry on—was there with "the priests, the Levites and the rest of the exiles" to dedicate the new structure to the God who had brought them back from despair (see Ezra 6:13–18).

INTERESTING. . . Zechariah was not the only person to prophesy in favor of rebuilding the temple. Another prophet named Haggai—Zechariah's contemporary—also wrote and spoke to encourage the exiles in their most important work.

Judah's King ZEDEKIAH cries out as his sons are slaughtered before his eyes. It's the last thing he'll ever see, as the invading Babylonians will shortly gouge out his eyes.

# ZEDEKIAH
## King of Judah

[Nebuchadnezzar] made Mattaniah, Jehoiachin's uncle,
king in his place and changed his name to Zedekiah.

2 KINGS 24:17

A word of advice: If you are the king of a small nation and you were put on the throne by the king of a much bigger, more powerful nation, rebellion is generally not a wise option. Unfortunately for all of Judah, Zedekiah did not heed such advice.

Zedekiah was the last king of Judah. His nephew Jehoiachin had preceded him on the throne, having the misfortune to rise to power just as King Nebuchadnezzar of Babylon decided to lay siege to the city of Jerusalem. The year was 597 BC. Time was running out for the kingdom of Judah.

Jehoiachin was forced into a humiliating surrender, after which Nebuchadnezzar looted the temple and displaced all but the poorest residents from Jerusalem. Jehoiachin was carried to Babylon, while his uncle, Zedekiah, was made king in his place.

Zedekiah, however, had little real power. He did not even have control over his own name. That had once been Mattaniah, but Nebuchadnezzar changed it when he put him on the throne. It was a simple yet profound way of reminding Zedekiah who was in charge.

Zedekiah ruled for just over a decade, and then he made the biggest mistake of his life: He rebelled against the king of Babylon. It seems that Zedekiah did not bother to seek God's direction until well after he had committed to revolt. Only when Nebuchadnezzar was beating down Jerusalem's door did the king of Judah seek advice from the prophet Jeremiah (see Jeremiah 21). Unfortunately, Jeremiah had no words of encouragement for Zedekiah. Time was up. Zedekiah and his people had nothing to look forward to but "plague, sword and famine"— and finally, total defeat at the hands of the Babylonian army.

As a final insult, Zedekiah was forced to watch as his sons were killed. Then his eyes were gouged out, and he was led to Babylon.

INTERESTING. . . Like Jeremiah, the prophet Ezekiel had anything but kind words for Zedekiah (see Ezekiel 17:14–16). Ezekiel seemed to marvel at Zedekiah's stupidity, noting with astonishment that it was after Nebuchadnezzar had rendered Judah "unable to rise again" that Zedekiah chose to rebel. "Will he succeed?" Ezekiel asked, his words no doubt dripping with sarcasm. "Will he break the treaty and yet escape?" The answer was a resounding no.

# ZEPHANIAH
## Prophet of Noble Heritage

The LORD within her is righteous; he does no wrong. Morning by morning
he dispenses his justice, and every new day he does not fail,
yet the unrighteous know no shame.
ZEPHANIAH 3:5

The prophet Zephaniah was not afraid to speak truth to those in power, which is
especially remarkable, considering his royal pedigree.

Other prophets had introduced themselves by identifying their fathers and
perhaps even their grandfathers (see, for example, Zechariah 1:1). Zephaniah,
however, felt the need to trace four generations of ancestors in his introduc-
tion—and for good reason, too. Zephaniah's great-great-grandfather was Hezekiah, one of Judah's most celebrated kings. Hezekiah was judged to be uniquely
devoted to God. According to the writer of 2 Kings, "There was no one like him
among all the kings of Judah, either before him or after him" (2 Kings 18:5). It is
no wonder that Zephaniah identified himself with Hezekiah—it was a powerful
means of establishing his credibility.

It also connected him very closely to his audience. Zephaniah prophesied
during the reign of Josiah, great-grandson of Hezekiah and the last good king
of Judah. In other words, Zephaniah and Josiah were relatives. This fact made
Zephaniah's prophecy against Judah and "the king's sons" in particular even more
daring (see Zephaniah 1:4–8).

Zephaniah described an imminent judgment, which he called the "day of
the Lord" (see, for example, Zephaniah 1:14). It was to be a day on which nothing could save the people of Judah—or "all who live in the earth," for that matter
(see Zephaniah 1:18).

But Zephaniah also spoke of hope—of a day when the people's lips would
be purified and they would once again call on God (see Zephaniah 3:9). By
this time, Jerusalem's fate had been sealed, but perhaps Zephaniah took heart at
Josiah's reforms and was able to foresee a day when God would once again take
"great delight" in His people (Zephaniah 3:17).

INTERESTING. . . Zephaniah's name means either "the Lord
has treasured" or "the Lord has hidden," leading some scholars
to suggest that Zephaniah may have been born during the reign
of Hezekiah's son Manasseh. Manasseh was said to have shed an
unthinkable amount of innocent blood (see 2 Kings 21:16).

# ZIPPORAH
## Wife of Moses

Moses was willing to dwell with the man,
and he gave his daughter Zipporah to Moses.
EXODUS 2:21 NASB

Zipporah's appearance in the Bible's story line begins with murder. She neither witnessed nor participated in the slaying, but she enters the biblical narrative when she marries a fugitive wanted for murder: Moses.

Moses' name usually invokes the image of a bold leader and spiritual giant, but that wasn't always the case. At one time, Moses lived the life of an adopted prince in Pharaoh's palace. Then one day, Moses murdered an Egyptian for abusing a Hebrew slave. Though Moses tried to hide his crime by burying the body, Pharaoh heard what Moses had done, and the future Bible hero became an outlaw (Exodus 2).

After running over a hundred miles, Moses made it to the land of Midian, located east of the Sinai Peninsula. While resting there, he saw seven sisters, caring for their flock, fighting the harmful treatment of other shepherds. Seeing their trouble, Moses chased off their abusers and proceeded to water the sisters' flock. Their father, Jethro, rewarded Moses' kindness by inviting him to live with them and by ultimately giving his daughter Zipporah to him in marriage. Together, Moses and Zipporah had two sons, named Gershom and Eliezer.

To survive as a shepherdess in the desert region of Midian, Zipporah must have been an industrious and resourceful woman. Those survival skills would have served her and Moses well as they lived together in the desert of Midian for forty years. These decades provided essential training for the overwhelming task that lay ahead: successfully leading the people of Israel through the desert to the Promised Land.

INTERESTING. . . Moses was about forty years old when he fled from Pharaoh's palace. He lived in Midian for approximately forty years and returned to lead God's people to the Promised Land at age eighty. After leading the people through the desert for forty years, Moses died at the age of 120.

# SCRIPTURE INDEX

# ART CREDITS

Andreas F. Borchert/WM 23
Bizzell Bible Collection, University of Oklahoma Libraries 81
cjh1452000/WM 209
Dennis Jarvis/Flickr 219
Dover Publications, Inc. 124, 137
Google Art Project/WM 72, 142, 150, 182, 272
Haffitt/WM 42
Jastrow/WM 10
Michael Wal/WM 121
Rama/WM 177
Robert Scarth/Flickr 192
Shutterstock 19, 24, 28, 35, 54, 60, 65, 69, 84, 90, 103, 105, 116, 156, 160, 167,
     172, 174, 184, 186, 190, 196, 205, 211, 223, 226, 228, 239, 242, 255, 258, 264
StAnselm/WM 47
Stefano Bistolfi/WM 140
TheBiblePeople.com 98, 148, 154, 260, 266
The Yorck Project/WM 134, 180, 234, 253, 270
WikiMedia 15, 21, 37, 40, 50, 52, 57, 63, 74, 76, 86, 88, 96, 113, 118, 126, 128,
     144, 146, 152, 170, 198, 207, 212, 224, 230, 237, 246, 249, 263, 277, 280
Wolfgang Sauber/WM 165, 188


WM=WikiMedia